ESSAYS ON INDIAN TOPICS

ESSAYS ON INDIAN TOPICS

THEODORE BECK

GYAN

Published by

Gyan Publishing House
5, Ansari Road
Daryaganj, New Delhi-110002
Phone: 011-47034999, 9811692060
E-mail: books@gyanbooks.com

Distribution Network
gyanbooks.com
India, USA, Canada, UK, Australia

ISBN: 978-93-7014-186-5 (PB)

First Published, 1888

2nd Impression 2025

Printed at: Gyan Press, Delhi.

ESSAYS ON INDIAN TOPICS

Arthur THEODORE BECK

ESSAYS ON INDIAN TOPICS.

BY

THEODORE BECK,

PRINCIPAL OF THE MAHOMEDAN ANGLO-ORIENTAL COLLEGE, ALIGARH.

(Reprinted from the "Pioneer" and other papers).

ALLAHABAD:

PRINTED AT THE PIONEER PRESS.

1888.

THIS LITTLE BOOK

I DEDICATE

TO

MY FATHER AND MOTHER

AS A MARK OF

RESPECT AND AFFECTION.

CONTENTS.

Page.

PREFACE.

The essays which are reprinted in this book are offered the public, not as forming a compilation of any intrinsic value, but as contributing to the discussion of current political topics. Indian questions will bear being looked at from a good many points of view. One point of view is that of the Member of Parliament at Westminster; another is that of the Anglo-Indian official; another, that of the Anglicised Native of the Presidency Towns; and another, that of the thorough-going old-fashioned Oriental. The standpoint of the writer of these amoteur essays is that of an unofficial Englishman, whose work and whose tastes bring him into frequent contact with Oriental society. He speaks as one who prefers living in India to living in Anglo-India, but whose sympathies with the wild theories of doctrinaire politicians are much affected by the fact that he has a throat that may be cut. In this respect, as an Anglo-Indian, he stands at a disadvantage with English theorists on Indian politics. For he can hardly hope to attain to the impartiality and serenity of the English Indo-politician, who, sitting in his comfortable arm-chair, can draw up paper constitutions for India, unbiassed by the dread lest his wife and children should be butchered, or the labours of his life for the improvement of the people around him, his town or his country, should be swept into nothingness by an overwhelming deluge.

HYDERABAD.

[BY A VISITOR].

MOST Englishmen confess to a sense of disappointment when they make their acquaintance with the "Gorgeous East." They have heard, perhaps, in their childhood of the Great Moghul, and of marble palaces and priceless jewels. If they chance to have studied Indian history, and to have formed in their minds pictures of the fine civilisation of the Mahomedan Emperors—the bravery and chivalry of the nobles; the graceful wit of the men of learning; the large, varied, cultivated and courteous society, resplendent through its taste, famous for its hospitality—they may have hoped, not unreasonably perhaps, when pæans are sung daily to the progress the country is making, to find society answering to their romantic conceptions. Suppose them to have come to the modern capital of Hindustan proper. Thatched bungalows and garden parties, society gossip and the dull routine of official life—it is not in English society that the imagination will regale itself on the hoped-for feast. If we look about for native society, there are the pleaders of the High Court, many rich banias, and the invading crowd of clerks in their *dhotis* from the Imperial capital; but magnificence, gallantry, learning and wit we look for in vain. Scepticism steals on the disappointed mind, the tales of the past seem a traveller's myth or a historian's fable: until the actual seats of the old Government be visited, and then the dazzling glory of the Moghul buildings, even as they remain, removes all doubt that the race that erected them were not, as some people fancy the people of India to be, semi-barbarians requiring State education to give them any aspirations, but were worthy descendants of the great Caliphs and Sultans, whose fame and whose doings have kindled the imagination of Europe. If one turns round now to see the modern Hindustani Musalmans, one would need to look closely to assure oneself that they are really the inheritors of that old civilisation. There is a tale that in the recent Mohurrum riots at Delhi a rich Hindu was stopped in his carriage by some Mahomedans. To escape, he told them he was a Musalman. "Oh, no," they replied; "there are no Musalmans in Delhi rich enough to drive about in good carriages." Here and there may be found a small knot of learned men. Here and there is a noble old country family that has not fallen into the clutches of the money-lenders. But, speaking generally, the community is passing through an ordeal of poverty that must end either in the extinction of their civilisation and political influence, or in the awakening of their minds to the necessity of adopting the modern methods of thought, which alone can secure progress under a Western Government.

While, however, Upper India shows no living remnant of her ancient greatness, there is still left in the Deccan a kingdom that dates back from the days of Mahomedan ascendancy, and that preserves in some degree the aspect of the past. True, you will find nothing in Hyderabad of that consummate taste in architecture which the earliest bringers of a new civilisation took with them into India and perfected during five centuries; for except for the singular form of mosque that adorns the city—a form which, while possessing no domes and in other respects far inferior to the Northern mosque, has yet an individuality and a charm of its own—there is less of living art than may be found in the bazaars of Upper India. Nor have the soldiers who accompanied Asaf Jah to the Deccan, and their descendants, ever made of their capital a seat of learning, such as even to this day Lucknow remains. But, in spite of this, the visitor to this most interesting of modern Indian towns will find that the traditional magnificence of the East is still not extinct in India, and that the race which did such wonders in the past has kept for itself a corner in which to display the pomp and hospitality for which it is famous. These facts give to Hyderabad a unique attraction for those who find the only way to enjoy a full life in the East is by studying it, and justify, it is hoped, the recording by a casual visitor of impressions which lay no pretensions to profundity. Furthermore, as this Oriental State is an integral part of the British Empire and is overshadowed by the British influence, we find many of the same social and political problems arising as in British India, and may discover side-lights thrown on them of a most instructive nature. For an occasional digression on such problems no apology will be offered.

The surroundings of Hyderabad are more striking than those of the cities that lie in the Gangetic plain. Hills covered with huge boulders, often delicately balanced on one another, break the horizon. On one the fort of Golconda rises high; below it are the great white tombs of the kings of the Kutb Shahi dynasty and of the dancing-girls whom they loved; and here sometimes on a winter night, could their souls be awakened by the sounds of sweet music, they might see Asiatic and European join hands to waltz in the spacious verandahs. Nearer the city the great Grecian palace of a nobleman covers the top of another hill. But perhaps the most attractive feature of the scenery is the lake by the road between Hyderabad and Secunderabad, which, with the ever-varying colours of its smooth or ruffled water, reflects with redoubled beauty the glowing tints of the sunset or the deep gloom of the storm. The æsthetic value of this great ornament of their town is apparently appreciated by the Hyderabadies, for they have made the road at its side their fashionable drive. Here in the evening roll by the handsome carriages of the nobles with the measured tread of their cantering horsemen before and behind; here the officials, dressed in the sober and elegant costume which the taste of the great Sir Salar Jung introduced, greet each other as their carriages pass, and exchange the latest news of the latest intrigue. The young Musalmans gallop by on their Arabs or Walers, sitting their steeds with an ease born of instinct and practice; Englishmen with their wives and daughters, and Parsees with their ladies in coloured silks, supply that element without which no scene could be considered perfect; and stout Deccani women water the road with their *gharas*. Passing from the lake to the city, we come unexpectedly on the centre round which the vortex of Hyderabad society whirls. Outside a modest compound, containing a bungalow that is a fair specimen of the *renaissance* style of Hyderabad domestic architecture, we find the road crammed with carriages; and our ears are greeted by the shrill sounds of the *naubat* that, like the bagpipe to a Scotchman, requires an Indian ear fully to appreciate it. This is the house of an Aide-de-Camp of His Highness, but the crowd of carriages outside and the number of distinguished-looking people within, some beguiling the time with a game of tennis, show that the Nizam himself has for a time taken up his quarters here, to be waited on daily by his officials and his courtiers. Into this sanctuary let us not seek to penetrate, but pass on, and driving in through a big gateway, erected in bastard Saracenic style, enter the public gardens, which are laid out in European fashion with artificial lakes and a bandstand, where twice a week those who love good music may hear it. We are now close to Chadarghat, a wealthy suburb, containing many houses of the Mahomedan gentry, into which if we peep we shall be struck with the elegance and taste of their furniture, in which they rival any to be found in India. The great city lies beyond, full of people from all parts of the Eastern Mahomedan world, each talking his own language, mixed up with the native Telegu. Here and there stand the palaces of great nobles with their interiors adorned in European style, with large mirrors and magnificent furniture. In the centre of the city rises a singular building, the *charminar*, with four tall towers, and near it the noble Mecca Masjid. While passing through the city and by gardens with waving palm leaves and goldmohur trees ablaze with crimson, we come to the Mir Alum Tank, scarcely inferior in size and superior in beauty to the one already described.

If the appearance of the capital of the Deccan offers much to please the eye, the social and political life is not less interesting to the intellect. In attempting any description of Hyderabad society, the first people to claim our attention are the nobles. As one passes the barracks in the city that are full of their retainers and meets the armed horsemen that escort carriages containing the infant members of their families, one is transported back to the Middle Ages. And, indeed, the inference is not wrong that these men occupy the position rather of feudal barons than of modern noblemen. For they possess enormous lands, and administer justice and preserve order in their own estates. The family of Shumsh-ul-Umra has an income of fifty lakhs of rupees. They maintain a private army of several thousand men. The position of the nobles may be likened to that of the Nizam and Scindhia, and the other great princes under the British Government. It is extremely dangerous for the Nizam to interfere with their privileges. Their high-sounding titles ring melodiously on the ear—Asman Jah, Amir-i-Kabir, Vikar-ul-Umra, Salar Jung, Munir-ul-Mulk. They have characteristic virtues and vices. They pay little heed to the Prophet's instructions in the matter of strong drink. But the worst feature in their society is their semi-barbarous zenana system. Unlike the Mahomedans of Upper India, they attach no importance to the principle of heredity as far as the mother's side is concerned. In Hindustan the good families pride themselves on the prevalence of monogamy. In Hyderabad it is considered very poor form to have only one wife. The strong mutual affection between husband and wife that is so characteristic of the Hindustani Musalmans is impossible when the lady finds herself only one among twenty who share the elastic affections of their spouse; nor can he himself care much for people who are mostly drawn from the lower classes, and have not been trained in those high sentiments which, however their intellectual education may have been neglected, animate the minds of well-born Mahomedan ladies. When a dutiful, loving and obedient husband is found—and such exist—his exemplary conduct is held up as a model in many a household. The evils of this system are so numerous—bad home education, deterioration of race by the admixture of base elements, encouragement of licentiousness, destruction of domestic happiness—that it is surprising to find so handsome a balance of virtues in the Hyderabad nobleman. Let us place his courage and manliness first of all. He is not like the Lucknow Nawab, an effeminate debauchee, but is fond of manly sports and games—riding, shooting, tent-pegging, polo—such things as become a soldier. He prefers horses to pigeons, and tiger-shooting to quail fighting. Here is a tale of a Hyderabad noble. His son had abscess of the liver, and an operation was necessary. The doctor proposed administering chloroform. The idea provoked the old man's scorn :—"There is no need of chloroform," he said: "he is my son. If you want to cut a hole in him, cut away. If he dies through it, let him die." The operation was performed without chloroform, and the young man never flinched. Then the hospitality of the Hyderabad nobleman is magnificent and unrivalled in India. His dinner parties are held in the gardens of his palace, which are illuminated for the occasion with innumerable lanterns, while, surrounding the *shamiana* under which the guests sit, the electric light throws its rays. Everything is done in the finest style, from the menu to the music which the band plays at intervals. At these entertainments there may be as many as five or seven hundred guests. A further virtue in the Hyderabad nobleman is the wonderful way in which he has shaken himself free from those prejudices against dining with English people and learning English which still fetter the nobility of Upper India. The objection to dining with Christians is practically unknown among the Musalmans of Hyderabad. Moreover, while the upper classes of Hindustan still hold back from teaching their sons English, there are in Hyderabad English schools especially for the sons of noblemen. Every year members of the Hyderabad aristocracy visit Europe. This means that a new and, it is to be hoped, invigorating influence is beginning to be felt. The originator of this social revolution was the late Sir Salar Jung, the great figure who, though dead, still overpowers with his influence the Hyderabad State. Certainly the Hyderabad nobility may boast that they could produce one man who had scarce his equal in the peninsula among Europeans or Natives. The able administrator and consummate diplomatist, who rescued the State from the confusion and anarchy that were on the point of engulphing it, and who knew how, in spite of immense disadvantages, to hold in check a big encroaching force—this great man, whose character and motives were as lofty as his ability and statesmanship were profound, has left the stamp of his personality no less on the society, dress and manners, than on the politics of Hyderabad.

Two facts in the social life of Hyderabad call for special attention. The first is the absence of that animosity between Mahomedan and Hindu which runs to such heights in British India. The second is the amount of social intercourse and the comparatively cordial relationship that exist between Englishmen and Natives. Confining ourselves for the present to the former, let us ask its cause. This is not an easy question to answer, and in venturing a few remarks it is not intended to do more than throw out hints towards its solution. We may observe, first, that throughout Native India, with the exception perhaps of Kashmir, Hindu and Mahomedan agree better than they do in British India; and, moreover, that as English education advances, the animosity between the two increases. That it is worse in Delhi, which has been English territory for a longer time, than in Lucknow. That it is stronger among those who have learnt English in the colleges than among the old-fashioned taluqdars and the villagers. That in Bundelkhand, where society is very old-fashioned, the Rajas are quite Islamised in their customs and thoughts; while in Calcutta, where English influence has been longest, the anti-Mahomedan feeling reaches its greatest height, and the object of the Hindu community seems to be to root out the Islamic influences that have been instilled into it for centuries, and to fix the ideal of their society as what they suppose it to have been in prehistoric times. If in conjunction with these facts the observation be made that this increase of hostility between the two rival sections is an advantageous thing for British rule, the conclusion seems to spring naturally out of these premises that the animosity has been fostered by the English with the object of strengthening their position. And this, indeed, is the conclusion that some do really arrive at. But a little consideration will show that the hypothesis is quite insufficient to account for the facts. It may be admitted that in the accounts presented of the rule of our predecessors for the edification of Young India, the historians have not been overanxious to single out the brightest features for administration; just as we should not look to Anglo-India for the most charitable exposition of Russian virtues, or to St. Petersburg for the most glowing eulogies of British Indian rule. We have no reason to expect a superhuman impartiality. It may also be supposed that the wisdom of the maxim *Divide et impera* has not been lost on the great Indian statesmen. But those who observe closely the effects of Government policy on the people will not credit Government with one tithe of the influence necessary for effecting so great a result. Government can collect a great revenue and wield enormous armies, but it could not introduce the metrical system of weights and measures. Its endeavours to effect agricultural reforms are attended with microscopical results. Moreover, from the way in which Government singles out the weakest and most timid classes for high offices, and attends more to the expostulations of penmen than to the wishes of swordsmen—as is proved by the concessions it makes in the matter of the Civil Service in answer to the demands of the native press and its unreadiness to gratify in a similar way the aspirations of its native soldiers—it would not seem that Government is very nervous as to the foundation of its political stability, and anxious to strengthen them by deep policy: while, last of all, the manifest desire of Government to prevent outbreaks of the peace, and to put them down as quickly as possible when they occur, argues the honesty of its motives and the wish to encourage good-will. Those who have watched the working of the District Officers, who, in the eyes of the populace, are the embodiment and incarnation of the Government, will testify to their earnest efforts to maintain peace between the two communities. The policy explanation must therefore be abandoned. The cause most generally assigned is that the Hindu learning history and reading of the oppressions his ancestors suffered under the Mahomedan invaders; finding himself, moreover, growing wealthier and more influential, while the Mahomedan is growing poorer; thinks that now he will have his revenge on his former master. The following facts are worthy of note: that wherever one community is in a very small minority and unable to pose as a rival to the other, there the animosity is but slight. And when there is a common head to whom all are devotedly attached, the sentiment of personal loyalty, which is a much stronger sentiment in India than national feeling, acts as a stronger bond. Such is the case in Hyderabad, where the Hindu nobles, whose ancestors served under Asaf Jah, would not yield an inch to the Mahomedans in their loyalty to the

Nizam. This fact should be taken note of by those politicians who think to create unity by conjuring with the word "native" and establishing as a cult hatred of the Englishman; whereas the only possibility, apart from arms, of holding the different classes in India together is by the growth of an Imperial sentiment embracing the Empire, to override and harmonise the diverse national sentiments that, though rudimentary, are daily gathering force. Some look to English culture for giving a common basis of sympathy, but it may be worth pointing out that Western thought tends to cut one bond that already exists, the *faqir*, who whether alive or in his tomb, whether as Hindu astrologer or departed Mahomedan saint, elicits the unbounded devotion of both sections of the community. It may be doubted whether a common reverence for the *pir* is not a stronger bond of union than a common acquaintance with Shakespeare. As a further cause of the antagonism between the two communities, it is possible that the social disturbance created by our promiscuous system of education, with our equally promiscuous method of promoting men of all classes of society to high office, may have obliterated the old aristocratic landmarks which gave Hindus and Mahomedans of good breeding common sympathies as opposed to the lower orders, and may have cleared the ground for a combination based only on common faith. If this be true, perhaps the Hyderabad school for the sons of noblemen may preserve the sympathy that exists between the Mahomedan and Hindu nobles, and so maintain a social barrier against the inroads of race animosity. But even in Hyderabad there are indications that the *entente cordiale* will become weakened with the spread of knowledge. And indeed, considering the immense strength of the nationality feeling in modern Europe, where it will thrive on the least possible pretext, as in Ireland—in startling contrast to India, where the sentiment of nationality is in no race strong, and political ethics put loyalty to a chief far higher than loyalty to a nation ; where, in short, personal sentiments are stronger than civic or national ones—it is only to be expected that the result of the introduction of Western thought and of Western political institutions into India will be to increase the feeling of nationality, not as the ridiculous pretence of some would have it, thereby forming one common nationality, but creating strongly opposed political units. Future history alone can show whether the existence of these sentiments will tend to mutual destruction, or by the peaceful rivalry they engender to the advancement of all communities ; whether or no ultimately, after the lapse of centuries, by the adoption of a common faith and free inter-marriage, any common Indian nationality will emerge in answer to the aspirations of those who profess to desire it. But, alas ! where shall we be then ?

The second social fact towards which we have drawn attention is the much more cordial relationship existing here between Englishmen and Natives than in British India. At the dinners to which allusion has been made, Native gentlemen take in English ladies, who after dinner visit the ladies in the zenana. The English Club contains many Native gentlemen. The English officers play polo with His Highness's officers. Cosmopolitan picnic parties are one of the amusements of the winter. In fact, as regards social intercourse, Hyderabad easily takes the first position among the cities of India. What is the cause of this state of things? Were an Indian Thackeray exposing the weaknesses of the society of his day, he might point to the fact that the Natives here have power and wealth, give dinners that would satisfy an epicure, and entertainments that no one would willingly miss. Did not the present Sir Salar Jung engage the best violinist that has been to India for years to please his guests? "Yes," we indignantly answer; "but the Natives here are really gentlemen, and understand English manners, and can talk as well as our own countrymen. We have not met people like them before; if we had, we should have behaved in the same way." Our social cynic replies triumphantly that many of these very men were once minor officials in British India, but that then as they were neither wealthy nor powerful their merits were undiscovered. No doubt when a man employs a first class tailor, lives in a well-furnished house, and drives about in a stylish equipage, his social qualities are more easily cognizable by the average man than when they depend for recognition on the human mind within. It requires some sympathy with Bohemianism to recognise genius in tatters. And there is very little of Bohemianism to mitigate the dulness of our society. We are too business-like and prosaic. And then, as regards social intercourse with Natives, let us honestly confess that the greatest barrier of all is our pride. John Bull on the continent of Europe turns up his nose at everything he sees; how much more in the East! John Bull with all his virtues and his vices—his probity, his energy, his self-reliance and his patriotism; his want of idealism, his inadaptability, his contempt of everything he doesn't understand, his social snobbishness—has put his foot down in India, and is proudly conscious of attracting the awe-struck and, he would fain believe, admiring gaze of two hundred and fifty swarthy millions. John Bull finds on landing at Bombay that his influence and his empire depend to a large extent on prestige, and he naturally wishes to live up to it, and having rather vague ideas as to what the prestige depends on, thinks the safest way is to show he has a full appreciation of his claims to it. Let us not blame him too much. It is a failing common among those who are born to rule. Dr. Fryer, an old traveller to India 200 years ago, says of our predecessors:—"The Moormen domineer over the Indians most insufferably." In Hyderabad John's pride as a ruler is not so excessive, and he doesn't feel he has that terrible prestige to support, so he treats the Oriental more as he would if he met him "at home." Nobody complains of John at home. Every Native who returns from

England comes with the tale that the English in England and the English in India belong to two different species. This is not true. No one who has not experienced them can fully realize the difficulties which an Englishman finds who attempts social intercourse with the people. Still the effort should be made; and, if persevered in, it will repay itself; while it would remove a danger to our Empire which many people think will ultimately prove fatal to it—the resentment of all influential Natives at the supercilious treatment of the English—a cause of discontent which lies at the bottom of most of the political dissatisfaction for which higher education is held responsible.

The second reason why social intercourse between Englishmen and Natives has taken root at Hyderabad is that the Natives themselves, being Musalmans of rank, are suited for social intercourse with English gentlemen. In many places no pleasant social intercourse could be established for the simple reason that the elements, like oil and water, could not be made to mix. It may be confidently predicted that the military man and the Bengali Babu will never be bosom friends. But the British officer, who, by-the-bye, has a high reputation among the Natives for his manners, recognises a kindred spirit in a man like Afsar Jung, who will look a tiger in the face as coolly as one might oneself a cow, and who for polo and panther-spearing has no superior in the Deccan. Looks also count for something, though their effect is not always to attract. When a young lady said to her puritanical mother—"Oh, So-and-so," alluding to one of His Highness's officers, "has such beautiful eyes, enough to drive any woman to distraction," the old lady seriously thought of decamping with her family. It is easier, too, for an Englishman to understand a Musalman than to penetrate into the recesses of the Hindu mind, though in very religious people this similarity of faith sometimes acts as an incentive to conflict. But there is not much religious bigotry among the Mahomedan gentry of Hyderabad, and as they are fond of horses, and a few of them like books, and most of them like dinner parties, and (shall we add) some of them like intrigue—in all which matters the local English community can furnish sympathisers—the elements clearly exist out of which to construct social intercourse. One barrier remains, though there are indications that that too will in time disappear. This is the *purdah* system, and, next to insular exclusiveness and prejudices against eating together, it is the greatest hindrance to social intercourse. When the ladies of Islam have vindicated their position, then may free social intercourse take place, and the Mahomedan community will realize that its own social life has hitherto been deprived of half its grace and beauty. So much for the social—let me now make a few remarks on the political—condition of Hyderabad.

In attempting some description of the politics of Hyderabad, it is not intended to discuss the abilities and influence of this secretary or that nobleman, such and such a Maulvi or such and such a Jung, as some journals that devote attention to Hyderabad matters delight in doing. Our envious pen shall not be uplifted against the happy mortal, whoever he may be, around whose house cluster the carriages of the great; but an effort will be made to describe the form of government of the first of Native States, and compare it with other existing forms. The Hyderabad Government is an Oriental despotism, tempered and propped up by British influence. The necessity of the sustaining power of the Imperial Government may be demonstrated from the historic fact that in old days, when the heir to an Indian monarchy was a man of weak character, a civil war frequently ensued, resulting generally in the establishment of a new dynasty. As the British Government cannot tolerate civil wars in the country, the necessity of its occasional support of the reigning prince is obvious. In discussing, however, this form of Government, the influence of the Imperial Government, and of its organ, the Resident, will be ignored, as this is exerted according to general fixed lines of policy, more or less understood by every one, varied, of course, according to the idiosyncrasies of the officer who, for the time being, represents the Government. We shall assume therefore the Hyderabad State is an Oriental autocracy, as if not a pure example of one it is sufficiently like one to enable us to understand pretty well the method of working of that form of government. And it is proposed first of all to compare it with a modern democracy, such as the government of England.

Among recent discoveries in the science of geometry a method, known as the method of reciprocity, has been invented, by which a theorem concerning points and lines in a plane gives rise at once to a corresponding theorem in which, while lines remain the same, instead of every point a plane is substituted, and for the plane, in which all the points and lines of the first theorem lie, a point in space is taken, through which all the lines and planes of the second theorem must pass. By this method we pass at once from one theorem to another of apparently a wholly different character, and yet the two are united in so subtle a manner that when the first is proved the latter also is bound by the sternest laws of thought to be true. A relationship of a somewhat similar character exists between an Eastern autocracy and a Western democracy. The lines which remain the same in both are the politicians, but instead of the point representing the king, we have the plane standing for the people. And it will be found that when a proposition about the one is announced, a second proposition will generally arise referring to the other, although it may appear in very different guise. And so, although the Hyderabad Government presents a much greater superficial analogy with the Government of India than it does with that of England, yet, to snatch the heart out of it and show its secret spirit, it will be better to compare it with the English rather than the Indian type.

Let us then institute this comparison. The main object of politicians in both Governments is the same, namely, office and the power it brings. The first step towards attaining this is, in the autocracy, by pleasing the monarch : in the democracy, by pleasing the people. The character of the monarch and of the people respectively are objects of profound study by those politicians who would be successful. It would be impossible to enumerate the methods adopted for acquiring influence with king or people, but perhaps the most successful one—the one that wears best, is most often useful and most reliable—is flattery. The greatness, the beauty, the ability, the strength of the king, are they not the well-known themes of courtiers ? And as for the generosity of the people, the nobility of the people and (who but a politician could have invented so glaring a paradox ?) the wisdom of the people, we hear these themes repeated *ad nauseam* on every political platform in England. Without any attempt at proof of so outrageous an assumption, it is said that men who are admittedly steeped in ignorance will collectively deliver decisions of the greatest value of the most intricate questions which not one in ten thousand of them understand. Your orator stands up and tells them so to their faces, denouncing as traitors all who dare to deny it. Is not this flattery as gross as was ever offered to a monarch ? But the ringing cheers of the crowd, coming as sweet incense to the soul of the orator, shew that the honeyed words have had the desired effect. As to the other means of pleasing, the gift of pleasant conversation is very valuable in a courtier, while for the democrat witty tales, especially if he has the knack of telling them well, are his most valuable stock in trade, and worth far more than profound political reflections. A judicious exciting of the fighting instinct may in both cases prove beneficial to the politician. An appeal to avarice is perhaps more useful in the democracy, for most kings have already got their "three acres and a cow;" while the king is more susceptible in other ways; for example, we never yet heard of a mob being in love. And, lest in all this something should startle a sensitive conscience, a doctrine is at hand in both cases as a salve. For the one, does not loyalty to his master justify everything, and for the other, is not *vox populi vox dei?* The first step having been gained, namely, the satisfaction of monarch or mob, what next? Now is the opportunity for blackening the character of the man into whose shoes you wish to step. In the autocracy that is known as intrigue, and will be talked of at length further on. In the democracy the members of the party out of power cast every aspersion they can invent on the character of those in power; make charges of stupidity and want of honesty which, from personal acquaintance, they must know to be, if not false, grossly exaggerated; ignore the difficulties they have had to encounter, and hold them up to the most unseemly ridicule. Each system has its characteristic vices. In that of intrigues, deceit and double dealing; in that of mob-oratory, cant and dishonesty of opinion. And in both systems are to be found men who despise these artifices, and who walk straight in the line shown them by conscience regardless of the pitfalls into which they may fall. Happy is the country that possesses many such men, in whom patriotism and principle outweigh self-interest.

And now for a few words on the subject of intrigue, its aims and its methods: that branch of diplomacy in which the Englishman is a child before the Oriental, just as the latter would be in Parliament before the trained Parliamentary tactician. In Hyderabad intrigue is elevated to the rank of a fine art. "Surely those two men, who are holding such long and amicable discourse as they drive together, are hatching some scheme of mutual advancement," the ingenuous Briton might think, little imagining that they were deadly enemies who had dealt one another many a good blow, and knew each was trying to cap the last with a crusher. The general purpose of intrigue is to raise oneself and diminish the power of those who are in any way one's rivals. In the democratic system the animosity and abuse are open, and men are often better friends than they seem to be. The reverse is the case here. As evils attendant on this system of intrigue we may mention the following:—It encourages deceit and lying; it makes friendship rare; it overburdens the minds of individuals and of society with mean thoughts, like the gaming table entrapping the best intellects, and thus destroying free unconstrained social intercourse, the growth of literature and true patriotism; and it fosters jealousy and petty personal passions. For those who appreciate the game it has no doubt its attractions. They have no cause for complaint. They give as good as they get and, if sensible men, will take a beating as philosophically as a chess-player. They are not taken in by false appearances of friendship, for they know the nature of the mask they themselves wear; and so they escape those wounds to their affections, those disappointments arising from the ingratitude and insincerity of those whom they reckoned their friends, which are cruel blows to more simple, truthful natures. They are not deceived by those in whom they put their trust, because they are wise enough to be very cautious in trusting anybody but themselves. On the other hand, those who have other tastes in life; who love society, or letters, or art, and wish, after honourably doing their duties, to have time to give to their hobbies; those who value friendship as the choicest fruit in life; or those who wish to reform their society and help the national progress, and who cannot afford the time to become successful in this kind of diplomacy; or who despise its methods and its objects—such people find this political system odious, and destructive of what they value most. "We left our homes to get a decent livelihood," they say, "and we must stay on that account. But the place is not to our taste. Better a post of half the value and a quiet life in British India." For in the Government of British India, in spite of the denunciations of the Native Press, there are certain advantages that are not fully appreciated until their absence is felt, and that enable the Government to buy good ability cheaper than any of its competitors in Native India. The first is the peaceful sense of security attached to its posts; and the second, though in reality the result of this, a comparative absence of intrigue. In fact, comparing the British Indian bureaucracy with the Eastern despotism and the English democracy, many considerations arise pointing to its being the most perfect form of government yet invented by man. The objection which our nationalists regard as fatal, that it is foreign, is beside the mark, for that is a necessity of the case; rather the argument that arises from the extreme foreignness of the governors and their ignorance of the people—an ignorance that, as far as their inner life is concerned, is in most cases never surmounted, points to the extreme perfection of the machine that can battle with circumstances so adverse, and at the same time get through its work at a much greater rate, and accomplish much more than the English democracy. This is the ideal towards which the Hyderabad State should aspire; but to reach it, it is necessary to cut at the root the system of intrigue by establishing firmly the security of the State officials. How can this be done? We have first to discover the cause of these intrigues which are not found in British India. The most obvious answer is that one Government is Native while the other is English. But there are Englishmen in Hyderabad,—and we need not be well versed in Hyderabad affairs to have ample proof that this explanation is quite untenable. Indeed, we sometimes blow the trumpet of our national virtues a little too loud. The Imperial Government, however, which cannot afford to have prejudices, makes no such assumption, and, rightly considering the national prestige, exercises a very wise supervision over the employment and advancement of Europeans in Native States, for sometimes proposals in these matters emanating from Native Governments arise from other considerations than those of administrative efficiency. One cause of intrigue seems to be the existence of an uncertainty at Head-Quarters: an arbitrary will that can raise one and lower another at pleasure. As long as this exists no real security can be felt. It is necessary then that those who wield authority should be, in the first place, strong; and secondly, should be willing to submit to restrictions on their own arbitrary power, so as to further the interests of their country. And for the enforcement of this there is needed an enlightened public opinion, recognising that the only right criterion of official promotion is the excellence of official work.

Leaving these very general considerations and coming to the more special features of the present condition of Hyderabad politics, undoubtedly the most remarkable fact is the predominance of a foreign element in the administration. Nearly all posts of importance are held not by native Hyderabadis, but by Mahomedans imported from Upper India. In a word, the Hindustanis in Hyderabad are like the English in British India. The analogy is very close. The reason for their presence is the same, namely, that they can do the work better than the native Hyderabadis. They were brought by the late Sir Salar Jung, and without them he could never have raised the administration to its present efficiency. Remove them, and it would collapse. They have mostly been trained in the British administration, and have learnt English methods of work. This fact is surely a hopeful one for the future, and indicates that in British India the people are making real progress. Again, the objections raised against them are very similar to those raised against the English. An agitation, and that, too, led chiefly by foreigners, either sympathetic or disappointed (how close the analogy runs!) has been started with the cry "Hyderabad for the Hyderabadis." They say the Hindustanis are undermining the State, though without them it would almost cease to exist. They say they have come to drain the resources of the country into their own pockets, and that there are plenty of Hyderabadis fit to hold the posts. Yet recently, when a Registrar of the High Court had to be appointed, a search was made, but in vain, for a suitable Hyderabadi, so a Punjabi was appointed. It is very strange that these Hindustani Mahomedans should be looked on as foreigners, because all of us who have read

Mr. Cotton's book know that the people of India, Hindus and Mahomedans, have recently become one nation and feel as one man on every political question ; and still more surprising when we reflect that these Hindustani Mahomedans share with the Hyderabadis the fervent faith of Islam and speak the same language, and that it is not so very long ago since the Nizam and his nobles came themselves from Hindustan. But whatever their detractors may say, the Hindustani officials of Hyderabad are certainly a remarkable body of men : perhaps the ablest group of Natives to be found in India. To begin with : their manners and mode of life are thoroughly civilized. They have among them men of great practical as well as high literary ability. Their experience of administration and heavy responsibility have sobered their views ; and they heartily despise the impractical bosh that streams from the pens of the graduate journalists of the Native Press. As for Parliaments for India, which is the latest insane proposal that our radical agitators have favoured us with, their knowledge of the aristocratic constitution of Indian society and the actual political forces to be dealt with, makes them regard the proposal with contempt. They have not even given their capital the inestimable blessings of elective self-government. Nor do they grudge the Imperial Government its summer trip to the hills, for they know that the best wealth of a country is the brain power of its statesmen, and that the country's best interests are served by maintaining that at the highest possible level. Again, the evidence given by the Hyderabad officials before the Public Service Commission was perhaps the most valuable received, their proposals being practical and moderate instead of doctrinaire and revolutionary. Among no body of men in India have the English better sympathisers than among these Hindustani officials, for their position is so similar to that of the English that they understand the difficulties of the situation of a governing class, while they have had that practical experience without which it is impossible to form sound political opinions. Their existence indicates the probability of the Native States proving themselves of great use to the British rule, by the formation in them of a conservative native public opinion to counteract the go-ahead radicalism of the Presidency Towns and the scribes of journalism.

In connection with the questions now at issue before the Public Service Commission, a lesson may be learnt from the way in which the great Hyderabad statesman grappled with the same problem. Sir Salar Jung chose men who united the qualification of having proved their ability in minor positions in British India with that of their being gentlemen. In consequence, with their greater wealth, their style of living has advanced to meet the requirements of their position. Unlike a certain native British official who, though drawing a salary of three or four hundred rupees, lived on fifteen rupees a month and employed his wife as his groom, their mode of life is such as to put them on terms of social equality with the noblemen of the country they have to govern. They form, too, a society which, like Anglo-Indian society, has the advantage of homogeneity and cohesiveness.

We care nothing for these things. With a glorious radicalism, which we are far from exercising in our own country, we elevate the commonest man who has crammed himself through an examination—a fetish we blame the Natives for worshipping, but who worships it more than Government?—and are sublimely indifferent as to whether he has those social and other qualities which will enable him to command the respect of the territorial magnates whom we call on him to rule, and who are the real leaders of the people. Perhaps if we realised better the social discontent our levelling ideas create in Eastern society, we should hesitate before applying to India the latest notions of the European political workshop.

Before concluding this sketch of Hyderabad politics, a few lines may be given to the present condition of affairs in the State. Since the great man passed away there have been many turns and changes in Hyderabad affairs. First, an old Hindu, whose grandfather had been Prime Minister, tried his hand and failed. Then the young Sir Salar Jung was appointed in the hope that he would emulate his father. His government, by reason of the support it received from the Hindustani officials, got on very well until serious differences arose between the king and his minister, which ended in the latter's resignation. Now, indeed, had it not been for a new factor that had appeared on the scene, a state of terrible confusion might have ensued. As in America, and to a certain extent in England, the custom has been for the officials to change with the chief; and on the proscribed list here would have been the very men who are most essential to the working of the administrative machine. The new factor that had appeared was an English Private Secretary of His Highness—an event which might have proved of doubtful benefit. But the man chosen for this post happened, whether due to the wisdom of Lord Dufferin or the good *iqbal* of the Hyderabad State, to be one who, by his tact and personal qualities, disarmed the suspicion with which his appointment was regarded; one of those with whose countrymen humanity at large disputes its claim to their sympathies; and who, mixing among the people with that fine freedom from insular conventionality which the great Anglo-Indians of the past exhibited, succeeded in inspiring in his royal master a confidence which guaranteed to the State servants that security of which they stood in need. At the same time His Highness won from all a reputation for good sense by choosing from among the nobles a minister well-known for his honourable and upright character. So, as regards the immediate future, the prognosis of the Hyderabad State may be pronounced favourable, though with a patient of a constitution so delicate, those who have its welfare at heart can never afford to relax their care and vigilance. As to the distant future, one consideration should be ever present to the servants and the subjects of His Highness the Nizam. The forces which brought the Moghul Empire to grief, and its offshoots in Bengal and Oudh, and those which operate to reduce the Mahomedan community in all parts of India to poverty, will act in the Hyderabad State also, unless counteracted by a new vitalising energy. Although there is no fear that the independent royalty of the Nizam will ever be touched by the British Government, yet, by the progress of the classes who fortify themselves with the weapons of Western thought and the insidious advance of the money-lender, the Mahomedan nobility will one day, unless they wake up to a sense of their danger, find themselves in the pitiable condition of their brethren of Upper India, when almost too late they are discovering their mistake. Let them reform their zenana system and return to a stricter adherence of the precept forbidding strong drink. Let all recognise that in education alone lies the future greatness of their country. Happily there is evidence that the Mahomedans of Hyderabad are awakening to a sense that they must move with the times. If they realise this fully, and bestir themselves with the energy that characterised them of old, there is every reason to hope that this living relic of the Moghul times may become the most sparkling facet of "the brightest jewel of the Imperial Crown."

VANDALISM AT BIJAPUR.

THE Bombay Presidency used to boast of possessing one of the grandest ruined cities in the world. Bijapur was in old times as large as Paris is now, and it contained more works of architectural art than modern Paris. It has a dome larger than that of the Pantheon at Rome. It has one of the finest mosques in India; and there are ruins innumerable, some of them of superb beauty, within the six miles of its walls. In grandeur of desolation it can rival Fatehpur-Sikri. Add to this that the art of Bijapur is unique. It represents a style of its own, a particularly beautiful rich variety of Indo-Saracenic that grew up of its own accord in the Deccan. All this indicate the priceless value of Bijapur in the history of architecture.

For two hundred years the buildings of Bijapur had resisted with fair success the ravages of time, and the worse ravages of destroying monarchs and barbarous hordes; but a more terrible infliction was in store for it. In 1879 it became the chief town of a British district; an English colony took up its residence in the citadel, where the finest group of ruins existed, and the old buildings are disappearing more rapidly and more effectually than they did under the hands of any previous barbarians. The old destroyers—time and the besieging kings—left marks on the buildings that added to their interest; but the vandals who are now making hay of them have thought only of utilising the masonry. They have built them into bungalows and kucherries; it is impossible to say what is old and what is new; the glorious art of the old architects is overlaid by the tasteless alterations of the modern engineer; and the whole has acquired an air of vulgarity that completely mars its beauty. The historic value is gone; but what is that? The British Government has saved some hundreds of rupees a month. Why does it not pull down the Taj, and sell the marble? Something *useful* might be done with the money. It is difficult to write patiently of the havoc that is at this moment being perpetrated. One visits the citadel. "What is that place?" "Oh, that," says one's guide, "was such-and-such a palace. Now that it has been made *durust*,* it is the Collector's or Judge's kucherry." Clink, clink, go the chisels of the masons, for though a large amount of damage has already been done, more remains. Surely there are in British India some traces of a public that loves art, that respects antiquity, and that will call out for the immediate stoppage of this disgraceful affair, and the restoration of everything that is not irremediably ruined to its ancient condition.

The first shock to his artistic susceptibilities that the visitor to Bijapur receives is to find the fine mosque attached to the wonderful tomb of Sultan Mahomed fitted up as a dâk bungalow, partitions being built up between the arches to make separate rooms, and the whole whitewashed. Wherever

* Correct.

nothing else in the way of improvement occurred to the exuberant imagination of the engineers who have been rebuilding Bijapur, they whitewashed the old places. So you will find the lovely little Mecca Musjid, built in stone, whitewashed; and the great mosque attached to the tomb of Ibrahim—a magnificent building unsurpassed by any of the buildings of Delhi for elaborateness of beautiful detail—you will find this mosque completely white-washed inside, and painted here and there with blue lines. And as to the Post Office, the playful fancy of our re-adapters of the masterpieces of the past to the material needs of the present has displayed itself here in all its graceful delicacy. The Post Office is, or rather was, a jewel of a mosque possessing all the peculiarities of the Bijapur mosque—the single dome, the strikingly graceful minarets, and the thick, heavy corbelled cornice. Now its beautiful archways are built up, and grilled iron windows inserted, a horrid tin sloping roof is stuck on to its front like the peak of an English schoolboy's cap, to serve as a roof for a verandah. The sacred building is full of clerks and covered with notice-boards, and the most sacred place of all, the niche pointing towards Mecca, has been fitted up with shelves for books and lamps and bottles. Add to this that the lower part of the beautiful stone building is painted a coarse red, and the upper part white, and a faint notion may be formed of the degradation to which this gem of ancient art, the like of which for beauty and true artistic feeling all the engineers of the

Public Works Department put together could not produce, has been subjected. But what matter? Probably the British Government saves thirty or at least twenty rupees a month. If twenty such heirlooms of the past be so *utilised*, the Government will save as much as the salary of a District Engineer. But, speak, oh, India! Wouldst thou rather have those beautiful monuments of art, those triumphs of human genius, those leaves in the book of the world's architecture, those living relics of a grand ancient dynasty, or the District Engineer? We complain of the Mahomedans for turning old Hindu temples into mosques. We cap them, we turn mosques into Post Offices. The Mahomedans pressed the old temples into the service of a purer religion and a higher form of art. In transforming they beautified—witness Ajmere and old Delhi In transforming, we vulgarise. The glories of the Post Office, into which this ancient consecrated shrine of monotheism, where those who are gone have bowed their heads in prayer and praise to God, has been transfigured, must be symbolized in a befitting way; and the tin verandah roof will, if it lasts, stand as a monument of the prostitution of art to sordid utility.

If one ascends one of the higher ruins and looks over the ancient city with its domes and minarets, and asks what the different places are, the same reply is given by the obsequious guide :—"That was a mosque : now it is a bungalow," he says of a building that has lost all shape and comeliness in the transformation. "That," says he of a large building in the distance, "is the pucca jail." "And that," pointing to a large dome, "is——Sahib's residence; and that was the Eidgah of Aurangzeb, now it is the police lines."

There is another aspect in which this business may be regarded. It is the taking of public property, or at least of what in every civilized Government should be regarded as public property, and devoting it to private purposes. The public is shut out from their ancient palaces and tombs; they are private residences, and are shut off from the road by gates.

I have only described a small portion of the wholesale vandalism that is being carried out. I might mention how a lovely old gateway is being built up and transformed into a church. The masons have been hard at work, and the painters are now daubing it with atrocious colours. But I will spare further details. The close examination of the alterations, the renovations, the brutal re-adaptations that are being carried out in this glorious old city—this ancient Rome of the Mahomedans of the Deccan—must fill the soul of an Englishman who has any reverence for the past, or appreciation of art, with feelings of indignation, humiliation, and degradation. "Do I belong, then," he will ask, "to a nation of barbarians? Has Ruskin's teaching fallen dead on the ears of my countrymen? Have the English in India no recollection of the abbeys and castles that are affectionately tended by the English at home?" Upper India has had its period of vandalism, but that was before Mr. Fergusson described the treasures of Indian art. And now the traveller who visits Agra and Delhi feels with pride that no Mahomedan Government could guard more tenderly the ancient monuments of Moghul art than the British Government does. A tablet in the wall describes how to Sir John Strachey India owes the preservation of these buildings. Bombay boasts of being an advanced Province; but unless Bombay bestirs itself very soon, it will be able to boast of having committed the most thorough-going work of artistic devastation that the melancholy historian of the future will have to chronicle, and this at a time when public opinion was supposed to be enlightened.

NEW INDIA.

THIS is the title of a book written by Mr. H. S. Cotton, a member of the Bengal Civil Service, professing to describe the change that has come over the inner life of the people of India during the last generation, and to dictate political measures necessary for ensuring the proper progress of the country. As the book represents a certain school of thought rather than the opinions of a particular thinker, it deserves a closer attention than might otherwise be accorded it. The political ideas it expresses are very widely held by the English-speaking Indians of the Presidency Towns. They are professed also by a certain number of English writers: some, men who have made a long residence in the country; some, who have honoured it with but a flying visit; and some, who have never seen its shores. The colouring they receive varies according to the experience and idiosyncracies of the author. In a book called *India for the Indians and for England* by Mr. W. Digby, the title of which the author appears to think enunciates a new principle, we find them in luxuriant inconsistency and but thinly diluted with experience and common sense. Another exponent, Mr. Slagg, M. P., perceived in the "National Conference" held last year at Bombay the handwriting on the wall in Belshazzar's palace, and hastened to make known his alarming discovery. In Mr. Wilfred Blunt we find some of the same ideas, this time with a strong flavour of the poet and breathing a fervent admiration for Islam; while in Mr. Cotton they take a Hindu colouring, and are tempered by the conservatism of the Positivist and by twenty years' experience of the country. As they are well presented, and may be taken as thoroughly matured, a criticism on his book offers a convenient opportunity for discussing opinions which belong rather to a party than to a particular man. The book in question undertakes to describe the state of modern India and to propose drastic political reforms. Having chosen so ambitious a task, it must be judged by its success or failure in accomplishing it. As it seems to the writer of this review that the present condition of India is wrongly diagnosed and the proposed measures of reform would, if carried out, bring nothing but confusion and disaster, he is obliged to condemn the book, much as he may admire certain passages, and grateful as he may be for the cordial and rare friendship displayed by the author towards the people of India. The description, for example, on pp. 143—152, of the contrast presented to the mind of the young Hindu by the idol-worship at home and the ideas instilled in the English college, is very picturesque and graphic. Mr. Cotton's speculations on the future of Hindu thought are full of interest. If the book had been called *New Calcutta* instead of *New India*, and had restricted itself to describing that section of the population which the author apparently knows best, it might have been pronounced a valuable contribution towards our knowledge of modern India. But as it professes to be a manual of instruction for the British public in political matters applying to the whole of India, it cannot be dealt with thus leniently.

The first obvious mistake in the book is a very common one—an exaggerated importance attached to Calcutta—a belief that Calcutta sways the rest of India, and hence a flattering assumption that by studying Calcutta we may read the minds of the people of other parts of India. Mr. Cotton writes:—"The public opinion is moulded in the Metropolis, and takes its tone almost entirely from the educated community which centres in the chief towns. No one can pretend to possess any knowledge of native feeling who does not keep his finger on the pulse of public opinion in the Presidency Towns. The people of India cannot but act and think as that section of the community which monopolises the knowledge of politics and administration, may instruct them. The educated classes are the voice and brain of the country. The Bengali Babu now rules public opinion from Peshawar to Chittagong." It may be concluded from these remarks that Mr. Cotton is not well acquainted with Upper India or with the Mahomedan community of any part of the continent. To begin with, it is a very erroneous assumption to suppose that the only educated people in India are the people who have learnt English. This is certainly most untrue of the Mahomedan community, for learning has been the heritage of Islam for ages; and although Mahomedan civilization has fallen much into decay, there are still to be found in India thousands of men well versed in the literature of Persia and Arabia, who would be recognised in any society as educated and cultivated men. It is a mistake to suppose that these men have no knowledge of politics and administration, that they never think about these subjects, and that they exert no influence on their countrymen. On the contrary, in logical thought and sound sense, their opinions often contrast very favourably with the utterances of those who are the apostles of the new school. Being the descendants of men who have governed a mighty empire, they have very distinct traditions as to the best principles of government, and the best means of captivating the affections of an Oriental people; and they criticize English measures from a very different point of view from that of Young Bengal. They have been largely utilised by the British Government in the administration of Upper India, and many of them hold important positions in the Native States. Their political thought resembles the old Tory school of England far more than the Radical, and they are by no means so enthusiastic for democratic measures as is commonly supposed by Englishmen. For example, most of them dislike the freedom of the Press, and think that it is calculated to fan the numerous race animosities of which India is a hot bed. On the other hand, they have their own grievances which find inadequate public utterance. Their first demand is for sympathy from their rulers, and that they should not be looked upon as an inferior race. They would prefer the Army to the Civil Service, and they feel it as a stain on the national honour that none of them are allowed high rank in that, to them the most honourable, profession. But in thought and feeling they are eminently conservative. And they are the real leaders of their communities, and command their hearts and their swords.

In estimating the political situation in India, it should be remembered that questions of Indian politics affect more nearly the fundamental basis of society than questions of English politics; and the first essential for a sound appreciation of them is to keep clearly before the mind the great physical forces which lie quiescent under the calm surface of Indian life, and which are the most important, and in the event of a disturbance, would be the only important factors to be reckoned with. Now the control of these latent forces is not, as far at least as the Bengal Presidency is concerned, vested in Calcutta. If the English left the country, the Mahomedans, Sikhs, Rajputs, and Jats would choose as their leaders men whose existence Mr. Cotton ignores in his book, and these people might begin to make things very unpleasant for the disciples of the new school of thought. To overlook this is to overlook one of the most essential facts of the political situation in India; in *New India* we may say, if by "New India" we mean not the visionary India of the future, but the actual India of to-day, the India we see about us with our eyes—

sweet and beautiful, full of attractive sights and of quaint old customs, and the home at once of two great Oriental civilizations, Islam and Hinduism inextricably mixed. But the term "New India" has an ambiguity which, unless noticed, is fruitful of error. For it may mean those political and social forces which owe their existence to English influence, and which at present form so small a proportion of the whole; or it may mean the India of to-day: and it is very easy by starting an argument in which the first premise pre-supposes the former meaning, and the conclusion the latter, to arrive at very fallacious, though often neat and pleasing, results.

The next subject I would deal with is the thesis of chapter I, that a common Indian nationality is showing itself all over India. English education, as the author points out, tends to bring the different peoples of India nearer together by giving them a common language and a comman culture. That this is a cause which ought in time to produce some assimilation of the different peoples of India, few will deny. But when he says that an actual spirit of common nationality is fast growing up, he is, it seems to me, going far ahead of the facts, and will certainly give English readers a wrong impression. The facts adduced to shew the existence of this sentiment are the common feeling among the peoples of India on the Ilbert Bill, raised by Anglo-Indian opposition, the ovation given to Lord Ripon, the protestations of loyalty at the time of the Russian crisis, and last of all, the mourning stated to have been general on the death of Keshub Chunder Sen. With regard to the last fact, he makes the following remarkable assertion :—"The natives of all parts of India, whatever their religion may have been, united with one voice in the expression of sorrow at his loss, and pride in him as a member of one common nation." So far was this from being the case that many well cultivated and very influential men of Upper India do not even know his name. What ignorance! People may exclaim to whom the name of the leader of the Brahmo Somaj is familiar. But the ignorance is no greater probably than that of the learned Brahmo's country-men of, let us say, Shah Abdul Aziz, the "Sun of India." These facts must strike one with surprise until one realises that not less than the physical difference between the burning plains of Mecca and the snowy heights of the Himalaya is the difference in thought and feeling between the Mahomedan and Hindu worlds. But we must leave this tempting subject and return to the book. The proposition of chapter I is thus stated :—"There now exists in all Provinces of India a national movement which is destined to develop and increase until it receives its fulfilment in the systematic regeneration of the whole country." And again :—"This growth of a national spirit marks the revolution which India has been subjected to in its political aspect." When a movement is dignified with the name of *revolution*, it is generally understood to have reached a considerable magnitude. It is not necessary, however, for us to bring forward facts to disprove this statement, for we have only to refer to another part of the book for a complete refutation of it. In chapter VII we find our author saying, "it is impossible to be blind to the general relation between Hindus and Mahomedans; to the jealousy which exists and manifests itself so frequently, even under British rule, in local outbursts of popular fanaticism; to the inherent antipathy with which every devout follower of Islam cannot but regard the idolatrous worshippers of Kali and Krishna. There are good reasons, therefore, for saying, as has been said, that the leaders of either community would find it insupportable to live under the domination of the other. Certainly; for we do not think that any amalgamation is probable, or that it would be possible to find from either community a common head with equal sympathies for both." And further, "it is only in the distant future that we can venture to predict a time when the fundamental differences between them shall subside under the impulse of a common faith." This is all very true; but how about the common nationality which is regenerating the country, and which has already made a revolution in Indian politics? The divergence between Hindus and Mahomedans is the crucial difficulty in the formation of this nationality, and though the Hindus outnumber the Mahomedans, the latter showed themselves for six centuries not inferior in physical force. Our author says, in chapter I, that a spirit of common nationality has made such progress that it is necessary to commence the work of political reorganization on this basis, and in chapter VII, that no union is possible until Hindus and Mahomedans profess one common religion. That religion, he indicates in the last chapter of his book, is to be Positivism ; but considering the tenacity of Hinduism and the shocks it has survived during the last three thousand years ; bearing in mind also the fervour of Islam ; and that in Europe the religion of Christ manages to hold its own against the religion of Auguste Comte ; the day of the universal adoption of Positivism, and therefore of fusion into a common nationality, seems far distant enough to allow at any rate the present generation of Anglo-Indian statesmen to leave it out of account in their policy. The only way of reconciling the conflicting statements of chapters I and VII is by supposing that the author considers the Mahomedan community not worth taking into account in considering the politics of India. But if this be his opinion, I venture to think that practical statesmen will take a different view.

In connection with this idea of a common Indian nationality, some interesting questions arise. In the first place, is it desirable ? This is very often assumed, but it requires some proof, for nobody wants to make Europe one nation. Then suppose it be desirable and highly desirable, so that it is an object worth working for, what are the necessary conditions of accomplishing it? It is quite clear that if there is to be a real approximation, every community in India must be prepared to sacrifice some cherished customs. Are people prepared to make the necessary sacrifices? We believe not one man in ten thousand is, and among the ten thousand must be reckoned Mr. Cotton. For what is a nation? The word nation implies that the people who compose it have some marked points of resemblance which differentiate them from other people. In a nation like England we find a body of men united by race, country, government, religion, language, manners and customs, and culture. In Europe it is considered essential that the people to be of one nation should be of one race, but in India we are obliged to make an exception to this in the case of the Mahomedans, who, if not a nation in the strictest sense of the term, are united by a feeling very like national feeling, and derived from the religious and social bond. Therefore to produce a nation in India of the European type, it would be necessary that for some generations there should be free intermarriage between all communities, a proposal which in the East would stagger the boldest man; while a nation of the Mahomedan type would require community of religion, manners and customs, and culture. In either case the people of India must be made really to resemble one another; and, to begin with, the Hindus must give up their caste system, which is indeed a barrier to a thorough-going national feeling in their own body. But Mr. Cotton, true to his Positivist instincts, is not prepared to give up caste, and urges the English-speaking Hindus not to abandon it. "That system," he says, "has its defects undoubtedly, but they are defects more than counterbalanced by the services it renders. Those reformers who are in the habit of describing caste as the root of all evils in Hindu society, overlook the impossibility of uprooting an institution which has taken such a firm hold on the popular mind. They forget that the attempt to abolish caste, if successful, would be attended with the most disastrous consequences, unless some powerful religious influence were brought to bear on the people in its place. They forget also that caste is still stronger as a social than as a religious institution, and that many a man who has entirely lost belief in his religion is zealous and tenacious of his position as a high-caste man, and scrupulously performs all customary rites and ceremonies. Caste is now the framework which knits together Hindu society; it is the link which maintains the existing religious system of Hinduism in its present order. The problem of the future is not to destroy caste, but to modify it, to preserve its distinctive conceptions, and to gradually place them upon a social instead of a supernatural basis." This ideal is quite inconsistent with the ideal of a common nationality. For one of the "distinctive conceptions" of caste is that outsiders cannot be admitted, but must remain outside the pale. Another "distinctive conception," that in a religious sense the merit of men depends on their birth, is repulsive to Mahomedanism with its strong view of religious democracy. "We are all slaves before God," say the Muslims, and in the house of prayer social distinctions are ignored in a way they are not in Christian churches. For many reasons it is clear that the existence of the caste system, with its rigid prohibitions against dining together and intermarriage, is incompatible with the real fusion of the different peoples of India into one.

Let me now leave Mr. Cotton's description of India as it is and pass on to his proposals for reform. He has a whole chapterful of reforms into which I do not propose to follow him, as each of his proposals would take long to criticise, and many would require the qualifications of a specialist to form any sound judgment on. He has a long list of grievances against the British Government, which all tend to shew how extremely foolish or perverse all the great builders-up of the British Indian Empire have been. Certainly no one who formed his opinions from Mr. Cotton's book would gain the faintest idea of the magnificent work that has been accomplished by the English in India. It is quite clear also that if Mr. Cotton's ideas had dominated the policy of the Indian Government, the revolution he takes so much delight in would never have occurred. For he deprecates railways, which are one of the chief means of binding the different parts of India together. He even finds fault with Government for their educational policy, which, he says, has produced "an anarchy which it is powerless to remedy." But without it how could the Government have fostered the spread of the Western ideas which, "notwithstanding drawbacks of all and whatever kind, has proved of inestimable advantage to the country?" Mr. Cotton's testimony to the beneficial results of the spread of Western ideas is valuable because, as his book shews, he is well qualified to speak of its effects on the Hindus of Calcutta. In chapter IV Government comes in for violent abuse for its land-legislation, or rather not the *Government* — I beg Mr. Cotton's pardon—but "a party of foreign occupiers who choose to call themselves the State." Our author is also horrified at the thought that this party of foreign occupiers keeps a very large army, and appears to entertain ideas of fighting Russia if she come too near them—certainly a most unwarrantable thing for any party of men, foreign occupiers or not, to do, who are not a *State*, which Mr. Cotton seems to think they are not, though he is so obliging as frequently to apply the term to them. Then we meet with some good old stock-grievances, such as the excessive difficulties placed in the way of Natives of India entering the Civil Service. And finally, some wild proposals, such as one which is having a run now in "Young India"—to govern the country by Elective Legislative Councils,—proposals which are certainly subject to many grave and apparently insuperable objections that are not touched on.

But it is more interesting to leave these numerous and very questionable reforms, and to accompany our author into a dive into futurity, and observe the India revealed to us by his prophetic gaze. We find then presented to our admiring vision a number of independent States, over which, as in the Colonies, floats the banner of England. Mr. Cotton points to a distant future for the realization of his dream, but one not so distant as that steps should not be taken now to facilitate its fulfilment. In fact, it is clear from his book that he thinks it ought to come before the amalgamation of Hindus and Mahomedans. Bearing this in mind, let us look at it a little more closely. Mr. Cotton's idea is that India should consist entirely of small States, each with a prince at its head, with an aristocracy, a parliament, and an army composed of its own subjects. Taking steps to produce this state of things, he calls "political reorganisation." The first thing that strikes one is that it seems quite opposed to the grand idea of a common Indian nationality with which the first chapter opened. The next thing is that in an Eastern country no parliament would stand a chance of holding its own against a king at the head of his army, so the poor parliaments would at once fall. The next thing is that the different States would vary enormously in military strength. Bengal, for example, would be no match for Oudh, and the weakest would soon become subject peoples again, which is the calamity to prevent which all this elaborate machinery has been set afoot. Another point worth considering is that the great spirit of progress which English influence is breathing into British India, which according to our author has made the Presidency Towns the most important centres of thought, and which makes so conspicuous a difference between British India and the Native States, would be stopped, and India would return to purely Oriental methods until Russia came to relieve her of the responsibility of self-government. Mr. Cotton's method of disposing of the difficulty of the divergence of Hindus and Mahomedans is very curious. It is not quite certain what he means, for his language, which is generally very clear and lucid, becomes vague and ambiguous here; but I understand him to mean this: that the Hindu and Mahomedan aristocracies are to be sorted out into different parts of the country, and each given supreme power in its new position. So that India would consist of Mahomedan and Hindu States, the upper classes in each State consisting solely of members of the dominant race, while the lower classes would be mixed. The first obvious objection to this scheme, if possible, is that where the governors consisted entirely of men of one race, and the bulk of the people of another, no very great improvement, as far as national self-government goes, would have been effected. The spectacle may be witnessed in Cashmere, and is not particularly encouraging. Better one would say a mixed Hindu and Mahomedan aristocracy if the rights of the common people of both creeds are to be protected. But it is unnecessary to dwell at length on this suggestion because it is quite impracticable. "The British Government should extend a helping hand to assist this natural tendency" of the Hindu and Mahomedan aristocracies to separate to different parts of the country. I do not know in what part of the country the natural tendency alluded to is observed. In the North-West Provinces the prevailing natural tendency seems to be for the unwarlike usurers—the banias—to buy up and cheat out the noble old martial races, Hindu and Mahomedan alike, and to oust them from their lands. And this tendency, far from offering any basis for political reconstruction, is one of the least hopeful signs of the future, for the banias are about as popular as their brethren the Jews in Germany and Russia, and are absolutely without powers of self-defence. But as for the British Government, or, to speak more accurately, "the party of foreign occupiers" assisting this movement, bodily clearing off all the Mahomedans of wealth and good family, and importing Hindu grandees to occupy their estates and step into their social position, the suggestion is worthy of Mahomed Tughlak.* And when Mahomedan nobility have been replanted, how can we prevent the banias from buying them up again? Like that of the land the settlement cannot be a permanent one, but a fresh sorting out will frequently be required as after a communists' redistribution of money. Mr. Cotton's great complaint of the "foreign occupiers" is that they have interfered too much; that they have played too paternal a part; that their railways have been too great a shock for the instincts of a conservative people; but all that

* A Mahomedan Emperor who marched off the whole city of Delhi by force to the Deccan, and thereby caused infinite suffering and misery. His other acts were equally interesting and mad.

they have done would be child's play compared with what he now calls on them to do. The aristocrats are to be driven from the associations of home and from the lands their ancestors have held for centuries. And who are the aristocrats? By no means only the rich classes, for many a poor man has a far higher social position than his rich neighbours. But if the charge can be brought home to any man that he is a genuine aristocrat, he must be hunted out like a French Prince and transported. Mr. Cotton is a humane man, and would no doubt not like to see this done; but it is the logical outcome of his solitary proposal for dealing with the most obvious and greatest difficulty that besets his scheme. Like many other Indian reformers, he does not think out carefully enough the results of his proposed reforms. Although he shows in one part of his book that he has observed some of the salient facts of Indian politics, yet when he evolves his plans of reform he practically ignores them. He commences his book with an exhortation to Englishmen to undertake the task of political reorganization. But political reorganization cannot leave out of account the great hidden and complicated forces of Indian society, to the elucidation of which he devotes so little attention. If with easy-going assurance it ignore them, and beguile itself with the agreeable delusion that an Indian nationality exists when it is but a shadow, its efforts will be doomed to disappointment and failure. These are the things which make any radical change in the government of India so extremely difficult, and these are the questions on which we want all the light that independent and thoughtful men can give. Anyone who shall fully grasp all the different political forces at work in India, and point out in detail how better institutions can be created which shall meet all the difficulties that arise and work well, will have performed a service for which he will receive the gratitude, not only of the people of India, but of many of the Anglo-Indians whom, in his book, Mr. Cotton so unsparingly condemns.

In chapter III, entitled "The increased bitterness of race feeling," Mr. Cotton deals with a very delicate subject, the prejudices that exist in the minds of Englishmen and Natives of India against one another. A great deal that he says is unfortunately true: at the same time I do not think he has been happy in his treatment of the subject. For the first object of any man who has the welfare of India at heart should be to do all in his power to allay these cursed sentiments, which are the harbingers of terrible ill for India; to encourage good feeling by inducing each side to be forbearing and to do justice to the other: and not to embitter them, as I fear Mr. Cotton's book is calculated to do. What can be the good of raking up a paragraph from some disgusting paper, inflamed by the worst passions aroused by the Ilbert Bill, and giving it as a fair specimen of Anglo-Indian feeling? No doubt the English community, as a whole, holds aloof too much from the people and comes too little in contact with their inner life and thought; entertains an unfair opinion of their merits; is not sufficiently sympathetic with their aspirations and progress. No doubt here and there Englishmen behave with intolerable rudeness to native gentlemen. These are facts which Englishmen in India are apt to be blind to; which apologists for British rule are apt to forget. A certain merit therefore pertains to men like Mr. Cotton who shew this side of the picture. But they should at the same time state their case with proper qualifications, and point out clearly the natural causes at work which remove much blame from private individuals. They should first be careful to do justice to the very large number who are honestly and conscientiously doing their best for the progress of the country. Such men are to be found in every service and in all positions. Living often under circumstances very trying for men who have been brought up surrounded by the thousand intellectual luxuries of England, they unostentatiously devote their lives to the service of the people. In the next place, the causes that induce many Englishmen to change their manners towards the people should be pointed out. If a man does not strike out himself into the sea of native life, he is sure to come in contact chiefly with the less admirable characters in the community. He is beset by sycophants and office-seekers. He finds that to protect himself from the pertinacity of some of the latter, he is obliged to adopt a tone of rudeness he has never found it necessary to use before. India requires an Englishman to possess a graduated scale of manners adapted for different kinds of people instead of the simple more democratic manners of England. A dozen more causes could be mentioned, showing how the faults we complain of in the English community are the result rather of natural causes than of individual vice, and could be removed to a large extent if the circumstances could be altered. Again, it should be pointed out how a single bad instance of rudeness shown by some underbred Englishman travels up and down the community with electric rapidity, and creates a most exaggerated impression of the attitude of Englishmen towards the people of India. Again, it would be absurd to put the blame for this state of things wholly on one side. The people of India have as distorted views of Englishmen as Englishmen have of the people of India. The current beliefs of Indian society as to English domestic life are as fallacious and as calculated to wound the sentiments of Englishmen as the contempt of an ill-educated Englishman is galling to an Indian gentleman. A great deal of forbearance is needed on both sides. But very little is shewn by writers of the school of Mr. Cotton. Their idea of fairness is to turn round on their own countrymen and paint them in the blackest colours for the abhorrence of the English at home. It cannot be expected then that Anglo-Indians who cherish as one of their strongest sentiments a passionate attachment to their mother-country, who look forward to a peaceful old age among the hills and meadows and cities of their native land, and who feel that, whatever their defects, they are doing as much for the honour of their country as any other class of Englishmen, should accept with gratitude the writings of authors, one of whose main objects seems to be to prepare English public opinion to receive them with dislike and contempt on their return. No man is to be praised for abjuring sentiments of patriotism. A Mahomedan who held up his people for the contempt and dislike of others would be despised, not only by his own countrymen, but by everybody. We admire him if he tells his countrymen of their faults with the view of correcting them. But books like Mr. Cotton's are not calculated to correct the faults of Anglo-Indians. Any great reform must be made by an appeal to men's hearts. I believe a great reform is needed; but if it is to be brought about, it must be by an appeal to the nobler side of the English character, and not by stirring up just feelings of resentment. Again, nothing could be in worse taste than Mr. Cotton's allusion to the prejudices entertained by English ladies. A full statement of their position in India would shew their prejudices to be only too intelligible. But however that may be, the ladies of all races in India are naturally more exclusive than men in their ideas. And whether they be right or wrong, it is revolting to every sentiment of chivalry, and of tender regard for that section of humanity which gives happiness and comfort to our homes, to drag them into a controversy of this sort. I have spoken of the effect produced by this method of treating the subject on the people of England and on Anglo-Indians. It remains to say a word on its effect on the people of India. The best way to encourage good feeling is to make sure that people appreciate each other's virtues. The first thing for the people of England to do is to understand the virtues of the people of India, and the first thing for the people of India to do is to understand the virtues of the people of England. The spirit that both sides should cultivate is admirably indicated by Sir John Malcolm in his address to the Civilians of Central India.* "The manner of European superiors towards the natives," he says, "must be a habit of mind, grounded on a favourable consideration of the qualities and merits of those to whom it extends; and this impression, I am satisfied, every person will have, who, after attaining a thorough knowledge of the real character of those with whom he has intercourse, shall judge them, without prejudice or self-conceit, by a standard which is suited to their beliefs, their usages, their habits, their occupations, their rank in life, the ideas they have imbibed from infancy, and the stage of civilization to which the community as a whole are advanced. If he does so with that knowledge and that temper of mind which are essential to render him competent to form an opinion, he will find enough virtue, enough of docility and disposition to improvement, enough of regard and observance of all the best and most sacred ties of

* *Political History of India* by Sir John Malcolm, Vol. II, p. cclxvii.

society, to create an esteem for individuals, and an interest in the community, which, when grounded on a sincere conviction of its being deserved, will render his kindness natural and conciliating."

I have said a good deal about this matter. I fear I have said almost too much. And if anything I have said is calculated to ruffle rather than appease these pernicious sentiments of race animosity, I sincerely regret having said anything. It is extremely difficult to form a judgment on this subject, which shall give due weight to the innumerable bewildering facts that meet one. On the one hand, we find a strong universal feeling of discontent among all the races of India, and especially among the upper and more influential classes, at the attitude borne towards them by the English community—a discontent whose origin is social and not political. On the other hand, the easy explanation of simply laying this down to the personal faults of Anglo-Indians becomes more and more untenable, the more one sees into the situation. And inasmuch as the discontent has a social origin, it is perfectly clear that if a healthy state of things is to be produced, it must be through the medium of the English who come in contact with the people, *i.e.*, Anglo-Indians, and not by trying to ride roughshod over them by means of the English in England. The great result to be attained is that Englishmen, Hindus, and Mahomedans, may all alike feel they are component parts, and have a share in the glory of a magnificent and enlightened Empire. This mysterious union of East and West should be beneficial not to the former only. In estimating the value of India to England, most people dwell only on the material side. They point to the amount of British trade with India. But India might have a much higher value for the English if we knew as a nation how to appreciate her—a moral and intellectual value. It is the narrowest opinion of Western prejudice to suppose that all beautiful ideals, all noble and profound thoughts on life, all graces of civilization, have been collected in Europe alone. The East, which has given birth to every religion which dominates mankind, has yet, I believe, something to teach the West. In this age of violent industrial competition, of socialism, of communism, and of nihilism; of the decay of old faiths and the pessimistic wails of philosophers and poets, it may act as a soothing and peace-giving influence on many a mind oppressed by the fever heat of modern intellectual life to go to India, to live among its people, and to breathe in the gentle influence of ideals of life that belong to a far earlier but a simpler and fresher period of the world's existence. England need fear no impoverishment of her intellectual life by her closer union with India. It is the ardent aspiration of many Natives of India and of many Anglo-Indians that this union may become every day a closer one, and that the Asiatic and British subjects of Her Majesty may be united by growing ties of affection and respect.

THE NATIONAL CONGRESS.

THE idea of an annual Congress, at which educated Indian gentlemen from all parts of the country and belonging to all nationalities, should meet and discuss questions of the day, is a happy one. From the exchange of views of people engaged in similar tasks, or grappling with the same intellectual problems, useful suggestions and fresh ideas often emerge. The occasion offers, moreover, an opportunity for the exercise of hospitality and pleasant social intercourse, and, for the general public, gives a topic for conversation that tends to enliven the somewhat dull atmosphere of Indian politics. If, however, the members of such a Congress claim for themselves a representative character, and for any decisions at which they may jointly arrive the weight attached to the unanimous opinion of India, and urge upon Government the expediency of adopting their proposals for political reform, then, indeed, they invite criticism of a most searching character, both as to the grounds of their claim and the wisdom of their suggestions. The two "National Congresses" hitherto held have proclaimed as the chief upshot of their proceedings a verdict in favour of the introduction of representative institutions into India, and it seems to be a foregone conclusion that the approaching meeting at Madras will endorse their opinion. In fact, in the public mind, the National Congress has become identified with this political scheme, to a criticism of which the following lines are devoted. Now to many men this task may appear superfluous. The notion of violating all historic continuity; of expecting a people saturated through the centuries of its long life with the traditions of autocratic rule to shake off at once its old feelings and habits, and transform itself into a modern democracy; of assuming that institutions which work not without friction in those nations which are most homogeneous and have been longest trained in their exercise could be adapted to a population five times as great as the largest in which they have hitherto been tried, and as varied and heterogeneous as the diverse peoples of Europe, seems to many thoughtful men, both English and Native, so preposterous as to need no refutation. Nevertheless, it would be optimistic to assume that unwise opinions have no effect in determining the course of events; nor should we trust too much to the wisdom of our rulers in England. The giving of a parliament and an extended suffrage to Cape Colony, with a population of two Boers and twelve Zulus and other African savages to every Englishman, is an experiment in legislation so amazing and indicates so absolute a faith that the potential blessings of the ballot-box are co-extensive with humanity, that those people in India who hold views which, by contrast with the prevailing radicalism and so-called nationalism of the Native Press, may be styled Conservative and Imperial, should I think be more active than they have hitherto been in ventilating their opinions and pointing out the facts on which they are based.

There are, it seems to me, at least four insurmountable obstacles to the success of representative institutions in India: to wit, the ignorance of the peasantry, the absence of a class from which to select capable statesmen and legislators, the inability of a parliament to control the army, and the mixture of nationalities. First let us consider the ignorance of the peasantry. The essence of parliamentary government is that it is popular government; it is a device by which the millions of common men in a country control the action of the State: the will of the people is the paramount power. They effect it by keeping a check on their representatives, and so effective is that check that the eyes of members of parliament are ever fixed on their constituencies, and the actions of English statesmen are curbed by the effect they are likely to produce on the popular mind. The virtues of popular government are:—*First*, the great stability of the constitution, due to its being backed up by more than half the people; *secondly*, that the poor classes have a means of checking the natural tendency to selfish legislation in the governors. Does any one imagine that the people of India are capable of performing this political feat? More than 90 per cent of the population are peasants. Real representative government means government subject to the control of the peasantry. The Indian peasant is unable to protect himself from the exaction of his zemindar or the extortions of the policeman. Has he the independence or the wisdom to direct the affairs of this great Empire? The ryot is a man not without a certain culture of mind and of feeling: he has a wonderful knowledge of old ballads and of the mythology of his religion; but his ignorance of politics is abysmal. Clearly he could, through his representative, exercise no control over the supreme legislature. And if he could, would it be desirable? What would he do? Perhaps forbid cow-killing, and spend the national income on temple-building and religious celebrations. Certainly his government would be a government of ignorance and of superstition. It is, I contend, neither possible nor desirable that the peasant should govern India. And unless he exercise real control over the government, there can be no true representative government in India. It is conceivable, however, that a form of government might be established of an apparently representative character. By a limited suffrage, or by municipalities, men might be chosen from the different districts or divisions to sit in a legislative assembly at Calcutta, local questions being left to subordinate assemblies in the provincial capitals. This form of government, though not popular, would yet be representative of a small section of the people, and may be styled pseudo-representative. It is presumably some such government that the leaders of the National Congress wish to see established. Let us, by a constructive effort of the imagination, call it into existence and examine its nature. The class which it would in the main represent is the English educated class. No other class would be well enough informed to possess much influence, even if it were a numerically large proportion of the electorate. The government, therefore, would be neither popular as the English, nor bureaucratic as the Indian, but would be a species of oligarchy, giving complete political supremacy to a class forming a minute percentage of the population. Now the pseudo-representative government would lack the two great virtues of popular government which are generally held to balance its defects—its stability and its impartiality—while it would not secure us the efficiency of our present method.

First, as regards stability and strength, a prime requisite in an Indian government, it is to be observed that the English educated class does not at present hold in its hands the keys of the magazines of physical force in this country. They have no control over the native army, nor over those classes of warlike peasantry which form the inflammable material of the country. There are two ways in which a government may command the allegiance of the masses. The one is by appealing to them directly, as in England; the other is by reaching them through their leaders. The former of these methods is impossible in India on account of the ignorance of the people. There is, I suppose, no doubt that although Government may protect the ryots against the oppression of the taluqdar, yet in a time of civil war they would join his standard rather than that of the Government. They are, as they were at the time of the Mutiny, completely under the influence of their hereditary chiefs, who are Conservatives of a palæozoic type; and in some cases, such as the wahabis, of their fanatical religious teachers. This is a fact which our political globe-trotters rarely recognise. Familiarity with modern political notions, though ultimately a great assistance, acts at first rather as an impediment in coming to a true knowledge of the East, as it leads the mind off on wrong tracks, and makes it jump by analogy to false conclusions. But our visitors think otherwise. Flattering themselves that their training in Western politics gives them a vast superiority over residents of the country in appreciating the importance of popular sentiment, estimated by them by the cheap method of reading newspapers and talking in their own language to casual men they meet, they offer the Indian statesman many prudential truisms about the danger of resisting national aspirations, which, as they cannot look below the surface, they completely misunderstand, identifying them with such sentiments as are expressed at the National Congress. Thus Mr. Slagg, M. P., called the first National Congress the handwriting on the wall in Belshazzar's palace. Poor Mr. Slagg! It may be laid as a charge against the supporters of this institution that they encourage these pleasant illusions, not so much because they like to be thought terrible fellows who could, if they chose, by a nod raise the whole country into rebellion, or, if conciliated, guarantee its loyalty, as because of their great use in tending to promote the aims in view. To this consideration must be attributed the anxiety felt by men who otherwise show but little sympathy towards that nation to induce the Mahomedans to take a part in this annual demonstration, and thereby increase the effect on the mind of the untutored politician. Even as it is the National Congress dazzles the travelling M. P., who at once thinks that he has the whole moral dynamite of India bottled up in a room. As I said this is not the case. But so often is it stated to be by the Native Press and by Mr. Hume, Mr. Cotton, Mr. Lal Mohun Ghose and others, that I will give a concrete example taken from British India, which, in the spread of modern ideas, is far ahead of the Native States. The fighting men in the district of Aligarh, containing a population of about a million, are under the control of the following families:—The Sherwani Afghans, who settled here in the time of the Pathan Emperors; the Syeds of Jelali, a noble Shia family which has supplied many good officers, civil and military, to Government; the Lalkhani Pathans, converted Rajputs, one of whom was prime minister of a large Native State; the unconverted Rajputs, and the great Jat taluqdars. The chiefs of these clans, numbering, we will say, about two dozen, fine strong men, fonder of horses and guns than of newspapers and congresses, are all ignorant of

English, and some of them are bitterly opposed to its teaching, which they think destructive of the faith and customs of their ancestors. Of their children a small minority are learning. Probably the next generation will send their sons to school, and in two generations, or some sixty years, the district of Aligarh may have a landed gentry speaking English, if they have not been by then eaten up by the banias. To satisfy the aspirations of these men, one of which is for a military career, nothing is done, so much is our attention taken up with the attempt to conciliate irreconcilable journalists, mistaking those that wear the lion's skin for the royal beast himself.

The claim, therefore, of the National Congress to represent the voice of India we may dismiss as unfounded. We have shown that our pseudo-representative or mock-popular system would not possess the first merit of popular government—its stability: it remains to investigate how far it would possess its freedom from partiality. Now, the fact that the cry that one class should have absolute power begins and ends with that class, is no proof that it is less disinterested than other classes. All classes and most individuals love power, sometimes for itself, sometimes as a means of beneficence; and who appreciate it better or enjoy it more than we Anglo-Indians? My opponents may say that now India is governed by one class, what loss of impartiality if it be governed by another? To this two answers are open. Either it may be said that one of these classes is more disinterested than the other; or, the bureaucratic system in vogue may be pronounced more impartial than a representative oligarchy. The first of these answers involves a thesis as invidious as it is difficult to prove: it is better to assume that in any class self-interest is the rule and self-sacrifice the exception. But the second position is real and tangible; and I hold that if government by a class is unavoidable, the present bureaucratic system is more free from gross partiality than a representative one would be. Suppose India were governed by a parliament composed of, and elected by, the Anglo-Indian population: would it not be tenfold less impartial than the present government? Our Anglo-Indian statesmen, actuated by deep policy or by a genuine desire for the progress of the people who have been so mysteriously entrusted to the care of England, represent a policy far in advance of, nay that could be distilled out of Anglo-India by universal suffrage. How many native high court judges would there have been if it had depended on this vote? Or how many statutory civilians, deputy collectors and subordinate judges? Would the income-tax—that most just of taxes—have been imposed if either of the classes in question had formed the electorate? The absurd agitation over the Ilbert Bill showed how much bile could be stirred up both in English and native communities by applying popular methods to India. The first essential of the Indian Government is that, based on a true knowledge of popular sentiment and on an impartial regard of the interests of all classes, it should possess a strength that can afford to neglect alike the prejudiced suggestions of Defence Associations and the interested proposals of the Native Press. We have indications enough that the class that supports the latter is not without the human failing of partiality. Its ever reiterated cry is to open all civil appointments to competitive examination, *i.e.*, to take them all to itself. Any regard for classes less advanced is stigmatised as iniquitous. And as to whether it is phenomenally anxious to do justice to the Government that has called it into existence, let those who read the papers judge.

We must abandon, therefore, the hope of securing by the proposed system the impartiality of a popular government. We have now to consider its probable efficiency, and this brings us to our second difficulty: where are the members of parliament, the capable legislators and statesmen, to come from? No organisation, no institution however perfect, can be a success unless the human units composing it be each adequately equipped for the task assigned him. And for the government of an Empire, many men provided with technical knowledge of varied description, endowed with the highest practical faculties, and trained by long experience, are needed. Some people think the government of a country a task not beyond the capabilities of an average intellect. It is admitted that the engineer who has to construct a bridge, the lawyer who must master an intricate case, the doctor who heals the diseases of the body, all require a long special training; but any fool is supposed capable of constructing a State, of dealing with foreign diplomacy, and of prescribing for the diseases of the body politic. This idea is as prevalent in England as here,—perhaps more so; but luckily there is a large body of men of independent means who have been trained since youth in the art of government, and into whose hands the actual business falls: there is our aristocracy, which always produces a crop of good statemen and able diplomatists: and there is our enormous highly-educated and affluent middle class, which is the political backbone of the nation. Has India any such resources? Her aristocracy is, from want of training, obviously incompetent for the work, and she has no middle class like ours. Her ablest men are either in government service or in the legal profession. As these two classes depend for their livelihood on their work, they cannot afford to give their lives to legislation. Only when they retire would it be possible. But parliamentary government requires men to devote to it the best years of their manhood. A house composed of illiterate ignoramuses, with a leaven of superannuated Government servants and briefless barristers, could not supply the requisite brain-power for dealing with such matters as foreign policy, the land laws, the currency questions and fiscal matters, which tax to their full the powers of the human intellect. The difficulty of selecting a very few competent men for the Legislative Councils is a sufficient illustration. In a country like India, where highly-trained ability is very scarce, the State must make the most economical use of the materials at hand. And that is done at present by attempting to select the best men when young, training them for a long period of years in administration, and from these choosing out the most distinguished for the great offices of State. Parenthetically one may remark that there can be no greater cause for anxiety as to the future than the doubt whether the present method of recruiting in England for the Civil Service is furnishing us with the best material available for the manufacture of statesmen. From the facts stated above, there is every reason to believe that the first breakdown of a representative system in India would arise from the inefficiency of the governing body. But this difficulty, while at present the most serious, will, if the British rule lasts, be the first to disappear. In two generations' time it is not inconceivable that there may be an educated aristocracy, and an influential middle class grown out of the development of industry and commerce. And it will no doubt be the aim of wise statesmanship to devise some method of giving these classes, which will have the greatest stake in the country and be the best possible conservative force and guarantee of order, a part in political life without imperilling the interests of other classes, thereby satisfying their just aspirations to a greater share in the glory and prestige of the British Empire.

When we come to consider the powers of the proposed supreme parliament, and ask what its relations are to be to the British Crown and the English Parliament—whether it is to be entrusted with the direction of foreign policy or confined in its action to domestic affairs; if the annual budget is to be placed before it; what powers, if any, it is to possess over the Army and the Civil Service—whether, in fact, it is to have any executive authority or be only a legislative machine, a fresh crop of difficulties arise, one of which, the connection between the parliament and the army, is singled out for discussion. One or two remarks as to the position assigned to their parliament in the radical party's ideas will clear the ground. First of all the National Congress proclaims its loyalty to the Queen. (Wonder, admiration and delight on the countenance of the travelling M. P., who never expected such loyalty in a down-trodden people!) But as the Queen has no political power, this profession would not in the least constrain the free action of the parliament. Now, a purely legislative assembly, which would only make such alterations in the laws as are from time to time needed, the Civil Service and administration being left as they are, would probably not satisfy the aspirations of the reformers, especially as the executive would be able to nullify the action of the parliament by only enforcing such laws as it liked; nor would a parliament having no control over the purse-strings, for its power would again be a shadow. We shall assume, therefore, that the object of the reformers is a practically autonomous parliament, owning a nominal allegiance to the Queen, free to make regulations as to the mode of filling up the Civil Service (should it think fit to retain that body), and controlling the taxation and expenditure. The question now comes—Should the Army, too, be under its orders, or is that to be left under British control? If the latter, then foreign policy must also be excluded from our parliament, for no nation could consent to allow other people to make what use they pleased of its army, perhaps sacrificing it in some disastrous war. Therefore the twenty crores or so required by the army in peace time, and such further amounts as are needed for war, must be voted by parliament without question. Even then the position is ridiculous. That the British should sit aside with a big army, coming in when called for to quell internal disturbance, supporting a Government in which they have no share, and that but for them would collapse, and enforcing laws of the justice and wisdom of which they have not satisfied themselves, would be a spectacle so anomalous and so little suited to the self-respect of a great nation, that we may, I think, dismiss it and consider the other hypothesis, according to which the parliament is to have full constitutional authority over the army. But it is one thing to have it on paper and another to have it in practice. How can five hundred unarmed civilians control a hundred thousand armed soldiers?

This is the fundamental difficulty which has, however, been so successfully overcome in England that we are apt to forget its existence. But it is felt in other countries, *e. g.*, in Spain. In old India the civil was always under the military authority. Even in British times the army once gained the upper hand, and its generals received from Indian potentates those princely donations which enriched our Anglo-Indian forefathers—a clear indication where the real power lay. The safeguard in England rests in the fact that the people so passionately love their institutions, endeared to them by the history of centuries and by their close connection with the national honour, that they are ready to sacrifice their lives in defending them, and, if the army attacked them, would arm themselves and fight the army, as they did in the time of Charles I. Perhaps even the most enthusiastic of the advocates of the representative system in India arc hardly prepared to do that. But we have a still better guarantee in England. If the head of the army were to give an order that violated our constitution, the officers and soldiers would themselves lay down their arms. In India the strongest political sentiment is loyalty to a chief, and loyalty to parliamentary institutions must become stronger than that before the soldiers will regard defiance of a parliamentary vote a more heinous sin than disobedience to their chiefs. Such a sentiment can only grow when a strong feeling of nationality has arisen and the national glory has been always associated with the constitution. Time is, therefore, a necessary condition of its growth. We seem to have arrived at this dilemma. The parliament cannot exist without possessing control over the army, but the parliament cannot control the army until it has existed a long time. How the English solved this apparently hopeless problem, it is beyond the scope of the present discussion to inquire. Enough to say that in other European countries it has not been done. In France it is considered a wonder if they exist a score of years without a revolution; in Germany the parliament is not independent; in Russia there is none. And even in England, in Oliver Cromwell's time, the army became supreme and turned out the parliament. The conclusion of the matter is, that until India reaches a state so different from that in which she now is, as no doubt in a thousand years she may, that the utmost flights of the human imagination are unable to picture what she will be like, there is no hope of a supreme autonomous parliament being able unassisted to control an Indian army.

Leaving the main argument, let us make a short digression on the functions of the army in India. Our go-ahead reformers ask for its reduction; it is not easy to say why. Do they want to lay India at the feet of Russia? If not, it indicates but a poor appreciation of the basis of the political fabric. The army is the bulwark of our personal liberties; it guarantees us the peace and comfort of our homes; it is the great safeguard against internal anarchy, and we trust it may, if necessary, prove the scourge of an invading enemy. It has this double task to perform—the prevention of internal disorder and protection against external enemies. When people say that India is so loyal that the first task is unnecessary, they are talking nonsense; when they say it would be as loyal as this if the Queen's Proclamation were interpreted differently, or if representative institutions were introduced, or any other reforms effected, they are talking greater nonsense. However loyal the country may be, in a continent like India, there are bound to be rowdy elements—restless adventurers, fanatics, dacoits—who would like nothing better than a free fight. Now the core of the army, the portion that, under all circumstances, is absolutely reliable, is the section composed of British soldiers. And the serious question is—Have we enough of them in the country? My Mahomedan friends have often expressed grave apprehensions to me on this point. Brave Thomas Atkins! I confess to a feeling of emotion when I see him here, thousands of miles from his distant English home and from all who have cared for him in his youth, ready to fight and die that we may lead lives of ease and comfort. Another matter, I venture to suggest, is that it would do much to render our government popular in India among those classes whose loyalty is most valuable to us, and would encourage an Imperial sentiment throughout the whole community, if the native princes were allowed to furnish their quota to the army, and if some Indian officers were appointed equal in rank to British officers. Is it not an indication of weak policy, of lazily accepting shows for reality, that while we rightly enough pay attention to the aspirations and "grievances" of the educated civilians, who can in time of difficulty render us no assistance, we entirely neglect the aspirations of the army? Is it just? The educated civilians have been raised by our rule, the military classes depressed; yet we appoint the Public Service Commission for the former and do nothing for the latter! It is by virtue of the strong arms and brave hearts of our native soldiers—of our Sikhs, our Gurkhas, our Thakurs, our Musalmans—that the prosperous lawyer and the bold journalist exist. They shed their blood wherever the Imperial interests are at stake, not only in India, but in Egypt, or wherever needed: have they no claims on our gratitude? Must we teach the people of India that as long as they are patient and respectful, like the army and the classes from which it is drawn, they may expect nothing; but when they abuse us and our government and our women with the filthiest epithets, then we will attend to their wants? This, indeed, is the lesson the people of India are learning. We flatter ourselves that our policy contrasts very favourably with that of Russia; but perhaps we flatter ourselves too much. Have we really sounder political instincts? Are we really more liberal? Do we seem so to our army? We may give medals to our native officers: Russia gives command. We send our native officers to the frontier, and they find a Mahomedan colonel taking his rank among Russian gentlemen. In appointing high native officers, we should select young men of good family, and put them through the same training in Sandhurst as English officers; they should be converted, as the high class native can be, into thorough-going English gentlemen in ideas and feelings. I have heard it used as an argument against giving natives high posts of any sort that they are unfit for the work unless Anglicised, and if Anglicised the political advantage is lost. The latter statement is not correct. However much Anglicised a native officer may be, yet his name, his colour, the knowledge that the blood of his race flows in his veins, will produce the desired political effect. Let me leave this and challenge the Congress-wallahs with a fourth objection to their scheme.

This may be stated in the following proposition:—*That parliamentary government is unsuited to a country containing two or more nations, tending to oppress the numerically weaker and provoke it to rebellion.* It is well to examine more closely the action of parliaments. The ideal scheme of bringing together a number of wise men to give their independent opinions on every question of State as it arises has been found unrealisable in practice. The ministers must be sure of the support of the house during the period of their office, and this can be achieved only by their possessing a majority pledged to support them. Thus in those countries in which the parliamentary system works best, the country divides itself into two parties, one of which governs absolutely for the time it is in power. Where this is not the case, as in France, the government is unstable as water. It is important to observe that in England both the executive and legislation are entirely in the hands of the predominant party; and that the only effective check on this party's proceedings is the fear lest, by a number of uncertain voters changing sides, they may be placed in a minority in the next election. The great vice of party government is that party is often preferred to country. It moreover encourages ill feeling and unreasonable prejudice in one half of the population against the other, although comparatively few can say why they are Liberals or Conservatives; and leads even respectable and intelligent men into the grossest and most unjust abuse of their opponents. Even in the Bengal Press we could hardly find anything more offensive than a remark of the *Saturday Review's*, calling the members of Parliament who voted with Mr. Gladstone "a mass of human lees and dregs." Now, what would be the effect of party government in India? Let me take the North-West Provinces as an example. The two parties would obviously be Hindu and Mahomedan, for they exist ready at hand. Now if Liberals and Conservatives can be incited by party government to blows, what may we expect from an aggravation of the already strained feelings of these two religious bodies? Moreover, the Hindu party, being in a majority that would fear no change of religion in the voters, would be absolute masters, as no Mahomedan Emperor ever was. The temporary triumph would, however, be dearly bought, for people who believe themselves to be physically superior would not tamely submit. The case has already been seen in Ireland, whose representatives have always been outvoted by the English. The only difference would be that the Irish are guaranteed a certain number of members, while here, as in every district the Mahomedans are in a minority, there is no reason why they should have a single representative, especially as the English educated classes would have most influence, and there are twenty times as many Hindu as Mahomedan graduates annually produced. Already this is seen in municipalities. I think a rule ought to be made that in any town in which two or more nationalities exist in considerable numbers, the number of municipal councillors belonging to any one class should not exceed that of all others put together, including the English members. Otherwise local self-government introduces on a small scale the evils here depicted on a large. The action of a free parliament in the North-West Provinees would tend, I imagine, to exclude from appointments and extinguish the political influence of the race that were masters here for six centuries, the superb monuments of whose taste now remain as the finest spectacle offered the visitor to India—a race that still remembers the past, and that counts among its allies not only men in every Province in India, but the hardy Afghan beyond the frontier, the Turkoman, and the Arab. This would hardly be a wise policy even for those who are their bitter enemies to pursue. The growing hostility to the followers of Islam among the newly-educated Hindus is not an amiable feature of the times. Even those who most resent the subjection in which their race was placed by the Mahomedan should recollect that in the East the right of conquest is the right to rule, and that few powerful monarchs have been so generous as Akbar; and should reflect that the position accorded to the Chamar by the ruling Brahman was not particularly exalted. The above considerations will show why the Mahomedans took so little part in last year's Congress. It was not, as Mr. Herbert Gladstone informed the English public, on account of their backwardness in English education, for the responsible leaders, not only in Calcutta, but in the North-Western Provinces and Hyderabad, intentionally abstained, but because, having their own traditions as to how government should be conducted, they are profoundly suspicious of so new-fangled a scheme, and furthermore, because they have no wish to put a rope round their own necks and place themselves at the mercy of those who have hold of the other end.

The supporters of the representative scheme attempt to answer this objection in two ways. Either it is boldly affirmed that the people of India form one nation—a position taken up by Mr. Cotton in the beginning of his book, but repudiated by him towards the end, where he recommends a wholesale shuffling of Hindus and Mahomedans to different parts of the country—or it is said that common interests will unite the different peoples. It would be waste of time to discuss the former of these at length. Neither in race, which is of Aryan, Semetic, Mongolian and aboriginal stocks; nor in religion, which embraces the two extremes of opposition; nor in language, some dozen or two different ones being spoken; nor in law, the courts administering various systems; nor in culture, Arabic and Sanskrit representing the opposite poles of the Mahomedan and Hindu men of learning respectively; nor in traditions, the glory of the one being the humiliation of the other; nor in character, social life, manners, and customs are the different peoples of India one. Such feeling as exists tending to bind the people of India in classes is partly national, as among Sikhs and Bengalis; partly religious, as among Mahomedans; partly of caste, as among Mahratta Brahmans; partly of clans and families; and partly communal, giving a feeling of unity to the inhabitants of one village. The progress of European ideas will probably tend to merge the minor classes in broad national distinctions, and thereby intensify purely national feeling. Hence, as time goes on, this fourth difficulty will increase rather than diminish. The second position, that all have common interests, is difficult to prove. The only common interests I see are, *first*, as against the Anglo-Indian in securing appointments; and, *second*, against a foreign enemy. The latter has never proved a sufficient bond of union in India, while the former would almost disappear with the creation of the parliament. On the other hand, in the great question of government appointments, the different classes are vitally opposed, while the religious difference will always be a fertile ground of dispute. The conclusion of the whole matter is that the representative system proposed by the National Congress would not be true popular government, but government by a class; would be neither stable nor impartial; would be in the hands of incompetent men; be helpless before the army; and offer no solution of the problem how the different nations scattered throughout India are to live at peace with one another; but would fan race prejudice and provoke civil war. The idea is an importation from Europe, and has not arisen, as a natural solution of the problems before us, from a study of the facts of the country. If we are to copy anything from the West, we must compare India with the whole of Europe and not with a small homogeneous nation like England. Now, a parliament for the whole of Europe is an obvious impossibility. And the present political state of Europe, with all the nations armed to the teeth against one another, and engaged every now and then in tremendous wars which become more terrible every decade, is not the most attractive ideal to put before India. Rather let us have patience, work slowly and surely towards absorbing a larger element of the diverse native races into the administration, give time for the development of the splendid latent capacity of human intellect to which every generation in India gives abortive birth, and for the great industrial future which will raise India to such a state of material prosperity as she has never before enjoyed, and cast to the winds these ill-digested and illusory schemes, the realisation of which would be the triumph of anarchy.

SOCIAL INTERCOURSE BETWEEN ENGLISHMEN AND INDIANS.

To the Editor of the "Pioneer."

Sir,—Will you allow me to make a few remarks in critiscim of your leader on social intercourse between Englishmen and Natives? In that article you state that "the wretched and miserable difficulties about eating and drinking are at the root of the whole trouble." I do not agree with you in this. In the first place, there are thousands of Mahomedans in these Provinces who have thrown over this superstition. I say "thousands," but it is difficult for me to form an exact estimate. I have myself, however, dined with several hundreds. These men would enjoy social intercourse with Englishmen, but they cannot easily take the first step. On our part very small efforts are made to meet them, but if we wished it, this pleasant intercourse might be increased one hundred-fold. Furthermore, although not eating together is an undoubted barrier, yet I personally have found that human sympathies are not so powerless that they cannot overleap it. The world would be for me poorer if some Hindus, whom I call my friends, were not in it. I do not wish to blame my countrymen, for it is as natural that they should prefer their own society as it is that they should prefer the English costume. And I know there are a dozen causes which create the gulf, not the least of which is that some of those who swim across from the native shore have come for personal objects, which prove at last a solvent of all their friendships. The Englishman, if he wishes to taste the real pleasures of intercourse with Easterns, must plunge himself into Eastern society. In so doing, he must encounter difficulties and discomfort. But he will be repaid in the end. There are men of culture in native society, men versed in the literature of Persia and Arabia, who would be received as equals in the best literary society of Europe, whom no Englishman takes the trouble to know. I have seen it with my eyes. I put it down to indifference. "Can any good thing come out of Nazareth?" some think. Yes, if poetry be good, if ancient traditions be good, if that peculiar Eastern sentiment which has charmed the poets of the West be good. An Englishman would probably be dubbed a lunatic if he confessed that the only thing which made life tolerable in his Indian exile was the culture, the interest, and the affection he found in native society. Such an Englishman will, therefore, at most hint at his condition.

When this want of intercourse between the communities, or a reasonable number of people of each, is fixed on my attention, I often feel, with a sinking of the heart, that the end of the British Indian Empire is not distant. The evils that come from it are gigantic; the leaders of the people are disgusted; ridiculous, false impressions of Englishmen and the malign intentions of Government are rampant in native society; and the English rulers are easily hoodwinked, whether by a clever aspirant for office or a noisy National Congress. They do not see the real structure of native society, nor the terrible danger that looms ahead from the steady decline in prosperity of every martial race in India, and the rapid progress of the money-lender. Real social intercourse is the cement which would make strong the political edifice. I agree with Nawab Mahdi Hasan in thinking it the duty of Englishmen in India, or at least of the ruling section, to make some effort towards the patriotic task of producing it. I believe the matter is not so difficult as it looks. The English residents of Aligarh, for example, have shown that many people are glad to meet native gentlemen when they have the chance, and be friends with them. Dinner-parties, cricket, whist, billiards, penny-readings, &c., are occasions of this agreeable social intercourse. There are hundreds of English people who are ready to meet native gentlemen, if the occasion present itself. Some effort is needed on both sides, for while the Englishman has in his hands the power of initiative, the native has considerable power of making it impossible. And that is what the entire Bengali Press seems determined to do. A never-ending series of articles abusing the Government and every English official or private man who displeases them can only produce in the Englishman a feeling of disgust, which makes social intercourse with the gentlemen in question the last thing he would seek.

Nor is the modest request of the National Congress, that the whole government of the country should be given into the hands of the numerical majority, likely to prove a source of sympathy between the Englishman, Hindu and Mahomedan. But I forget. For we told that in an elective assembly, if there be one Englishman or ten Mahomedans, and a hundred others, it is as much a benefit to the Englishman and the Mahomedans as to the others. The assembly is a kind of paradise which benefits every one who enters it and all whom he represents, quite apart from the trifling consideration as to whether his side is in a majority or a minority. Therefore I will present my bow to that august assemblage, and not bring it into this discussion. If what I have said, sir, about an evil which it seems to me is of gigantic magnitude, and for which we, Englishmen of the present generation, are largely responsible—if it tend in the direction of lessening the evil, then I shall be a happy man, although you Mr. Editor, picturing me enveloped in *hookah* smoke discussing the manners of Islam, may pity me for a fool, and point to the manly exercise of the tennis-field and the subtleties of the whist table as the proper recreation of John Bull. But if my remarks, like much that is written on the subject, tend to aggravate the matter, then I shall be sorry I touched it. As one whose circumstances have compelled him to see more of the people of India than the average Englishman, I can only say that the effort repays itself, and that, incredible though it may appear, all degrees of friendship and intimacy are possible between the Anglo-Indian and his Eastern fellow-subject. Let me close with a line from Bacon :—"If a man be gracious and courteous to strangers, it shows he is a citizen of the world, and that his heart is no island cut off from other lands, but a continent that joins to them."

IN WHAT WILL IT END?

Jack Cade: There shall be in England seven halfpenny loaves sold for a penny. All shall eat and drink on my score; and I will apparel them all in one livery, that they may agree like brothers and worship me their lord. Go to Sirrah! Tell the king from me that for his father's sake, Henry the Fifth, I am content he shall reign; but I'll be protector over him. Now show yourselves, men; 'tis for liberty. We will not have one lord, one gentleman. Away, burn all the records of the realm: my mouth shall be the Parliament of England.—(*Shakespeare: Henry VI, Part II, Act IV*).

I.

As it is my belief that the agitation of which the National Congress is the visible head will, if unchecked, sooner or later end in a mutiny, with its accompanying horrors and massacres, followed by a terrible retaliation on the part of the British Government, bringing absolute ruin for the Musalman, the Rajput and other brave races, and resulting in the retardation of all progress, I wish to place before my countrymen the reasons which have led me to form this opinion, and to invite a refutation of the arguments adduced. We had a sharp lesson in 1857 about the inadvisability of not studying the undercurrents of thought in India, and I fear that if we let the Bengali Press and the Congress agitation go on for another ten or twenty years, we shall have as disagreeable an awakening as we had then.

There are two things to be distinguished in the National Congress: *first*, its object; *second*, its *modus operandi* or method. In its method lies the danger. Were its object not visionary and unattainable, but wise and beneficial, the danger would still exist, unless a radical change were made in the means by which it was sought to effect the object. But before pointing out the latent danger of the method, let me say a few words about the object—the proposed reconstitution of the Legislative Councils.

One of the speakers in the last Congress did me the honour of alluding to some criticisms of mine on the proposal to introduce parliamentary government into India. He said, and many papers which criticised me also said, that the intention of the Congress stopped far short of a parliament, and was confined to the scheme about Legislative Councils, and therefore that all my arguments were beside the mark. But I note in the "Tamil Catechism," printed at the end of the report of the Madras Congress, the following question and answer :—

"*Q.*—Then you think the Congress will really be of great use ?"

"*A.*—Yes, most certainly; for one of the best means of promoting the welfare of India is the establishment of a Grand Council on the lines of the English Parliament, and if persevered in and wisely guided and supported by the whole country, the Congress will gradually, when India is fit for this, be converted into an Indian Parliament, which will take the place of the sham Councils of the present day."

From this and a hundred other indications, I conclude that I was right in thinking that a parliament is what the promoters of this movement have as their goal, and that the assurance that the only object is a reconstitution of the Legislative Councils is the language of diplomacy. But I will leave the parliament aside. I will suppose that the ultimate ambition of the Congresswallahs is their proposed reform of the Legislative Councils, and that if Government suggested going a step further, every man who now supports the Congress would turn round and oppose such a proceeding as too radical. I will now discuss this measure, which its advocates complacently describe as extremely moderate.

The proposal, as formulated by the National Congress, contains seven distinct clauses, some of them embodying several distinct propositions, and to all these clauses and propositions six hundred men gave unanimous consent! In the first clause it is stated that the number of members on the Legislative Councils is to be "materially increased," and of these not less than one-half are to be elected, while not more than one-fourth are to be members *ex-officio*, and not more than one-fourth nominated by Government. In the sixth clause it states that "all legislative measures and all financial questions, including all budgets, whether these involve new or enhanced taxation or not, are to be necessarily submitted to and dealt with by these Councils." It will thus be seen that the elected members have only to gain one supporter among the official or nominated members to secure a majority and be absolute. The use to which this reformed Council is to be put, is thus described by Mr. Surendronath Banerji, the proposer of the motion :—"It is impossible to think of a domestic grievance, or a matter of domestic complaint, which will not be remedied, if the constitution of the Councils were changed and remodelled according to our programme. Talk of the separation of judicial from executive functions, why, the reform would be effected at once, if we had the making of our own laws. Talk of the wider employment of our countrymen in the public service, why the Queen's Proclamation would be vindicated to the letter (applause), if we had some control over the management of our domestic concerns (applause). You fret and fume under the rigour of an income-tax which touches even the means of subsistence, why the incidence of the tax would be altered, the minimum raised, if we had anything to do with the imposition of the tax, or if we were permitted to modify it (applause)." Some further notice of the magnitude of the demand may be gathered from the philanthropic froth of an English lawyer who is innocently trying to ignite the gunpowder. "The day will come," said Mr. Eardley Norton, "when an infinitely larger and truer freedom will be yours, when the great question of taxation will be within your grasp, when you will in truth realise that you have got something more than mere potential power, when you shall place your hand upon the purse-strings of the country and the Government. (Loud and continued applause). Money is power, whether it be in the hands of an individual or of a Government. He who has the dispensing of money is he who has the control of all ultimate authority (cheers). Once you control the finances, you will taste the true meaning of power and of freedom (cheers)."

Now let us suppose these Councils constituted, and let us suppose Government to propose a measure, for example the income-tax, to which these high-minded democrats object. There are two possibilities. Either the elected members support the Government, or they oppose it. It is pretty clear which they will do; but suppose, for the sake of argument, they support it. Is anyone so foolish as to imagine that it will be less unpopular because the elected members agree to it? Everyone will think that Government coerced them. They cannot take on their shoulders the odium and the responsibility which everyone rightly attributes to Government. Nor can Government shirk this responsibility. Now, suppose they oppose the Government. Is it conceivable that under these circumstances Government could continue to govern? They want money to pay the army and their servants, and the Council refuses them. They are to bear the weight of the responsibility; they are to protect the country from Russia; they are to prevent the martial races of Upper India, Behar, and other places from throwing off the yoke of the native rulers belonging to castes and races whom they despise, placed over them by competitive examination; and yet they are to have no power. The electorate is to "taste the true meaning of power and of freedom"—without the responsibility. Well, in this case of Government finding itself frustrated by the Council—the case to which Mr. Surendronath Banerji looks forward with delight, the only case in fact which gives any point to the Congress proposal—what is Government to do? It must do one of two things: either abolish the Council, or retire from the country. The former case will cause great exasperation; the latter we do not intend to do, nor do the Congresswallahs want it. The experiment of these mixed Councils has been tried in the West Indies, and Mr. Froude points out that it is one of the causes of their decline in prosperity. The elected members, he says, always vote against Government, and thereby the greatest amount of friction is produced and the greatest unpopularity of the Governor. In Jamaica, when Government overrode the decision of the elected members, a Negro gentleman, named Gordon, a well-meaning agitator, called a big public meeting against Government. The Negroes went armed. Some English soldiers went to see: a fight ensued, the Negroes began to ravage the land, the country was put under martial law, Gordon was hanged, and the Constitution was abolished. That incident gives a graphic picture of what would probably take place in India, but on a hundred times bigger scale, if this proposal of the Congress were adopted.

But there is a minor measure which Government might adopt, without such disastrous consequences. A change might be made in the present Legislative Council by which a small number of native members might be elected by specified constituencies, no increased power being given to the Councils, and no handle in the executive. Such a reform would possess a specious resemblance to the proposal of the National Congress, and it is not inconceivable that Government might throw it out as a sop. I venture to say that this would, in my opinion, be a fatal mistake. It would as much satisfy their appetite as a sparrow would that of a hungry tiger, and it would give a gigantic stimulus to the whole movement. Moreover, when there are so few seats it would be very unfair to give any constituencies or interests a permanent footing on the Council. The Parsees, for example, are a wealthy and important community. If they were represented according to their numbers in an Indian Parliament, then in a Parliament of the preposterous dimensions of 3,000 members there ought to be only one Parsee. The measure would be unfair on those who were left unrepresented. For the elected members would consider it their duty to push the interests of their constituencies. And thus the Government, too, would lose, for this duty towards the constituency would conflict with the Imperial duty which alone should animate the members. A further objection to this measure is that it would insert the thin end of the wedge for the agitators ever to hammer at, and it would disguise the true nature of the British power in India, which is, and must be, a despotism, controlled not by ignorant masses, but by the law of duty. A cosmopolitan bureaucracy, with the ultimate authority in the hands of Englishmen, is, it seems to me, the only possible ambition for the Indian political idealist.

Besides this main demand of the National Congress, there are a number of minor proposals which are some objectionable, some unobjectionable. I do not propose to discuss them, because they would carry me far away from the main thesis. They have to be noticed only as showing in a plain and unmistakable way one of the principles constituting the *modus operandi* of the agitators. The principle is this :—That the Congress seeks to strengthen its hold on the community by opening its doors to every kind of political grievance. Thus, while bent on one main object—to seize the reins of Government—it encourages everyone who cares for some other object to join and vote for the representative proposal, in the hope that the mighty uproar, when directed on his pet scheme, will give it a chance. The army was held out as a bait to the Mahomedans, but they caught sight of the hook. The unofficial Europeans and Eurasians with amazing simplicity have walked into the trap, and have of course been received with open arms. Anyone with a following and a grievance is welcome. It all adds fuel to the fire. I am now well launched off on the discussion of the method of the Congress, and I have to justify the proposition I made at the commencement of this discussion. And I ask now—What will be the effect of this? What will be the result of keeping open a great grievance-shop in this Empire? What will be the effect on the minds of people who go and listen for four or five days to glowing accounts of injustice and mismanagement, brought in from all parts of the continent; to the brutality of this damnable political agent, who "betrays his trust to his conscience, his country, and his Queen;" to the cruelty of the Government which causes "thousands of their countrymen and countrywomen to be killed every year by tigers and leopards" because of the Arms Act? And when you have carefully hunted out every grievance—and I suppose no one has no complaint—and have collected them and tabulated them, and when the whole year round the press reeks with them, and once a year all the grievance-mongers come together and blow off their eloquence, will it strengthen the Empire? It will be a great running sore which will never heal because the ambition of the agitator will demand fresh grievances as fast as any are removed, and he will create them if they do not exist. There will be no difficulty in this. In every country there are men dying of starvation; there are miscarriages of justice and acts of oppression—this is the sad order of this world. Who that has once seen the East End of London, with its million inhabitants sunk in squalor, dirt, and misery, their faces ingrained with degradation and suffering, can forget the terrible sight? Or the spectacle of our great civilised city at night, with the drunken men reeling out of the public houses and the brazen faces of the women? There is nothing so shocking as this in India. But suppose London were under foreign rule instead of being under "the most enlightened Government in the world," all these miseries would be wrongly put down to the foreigner, and the forces of anarchy would arise in irresistible strength. So it will be in India. The agitators tell the people that all their ills, the miserable poverty of sections of them, are due to the English, and that their nostrum is a magic wand that will set all right. The manufacture of grievances is already in full swing. The Congress could no more get on without grievances than an English political party could without a programme. For without grievances it would die. And the Congress has to be kept alive because, if Mr. Hume's ambition is to be realised, it will some day wake up and find itself a real Parliament.

I have now to discuss the spirit in which these grievances are laid before the public, and the means adopted for stirring up the ignorant. I maintain that this spirit and these means are disloyal and seditious. I must now define the precise meaning that I attach to the term "disloyal." For I shall at once be told that the raising of three cheers for the Queen is a frequent phenomenon in Congress meetings, and that many of the delegates not only say but feel they would be sorry for the English to.

leave India. Granted. To doubt the fact would be to doubt their sanity. But I still call them disloyal. If a boy abused and injured his father to whom he owed his means of support, I should call him an undutiful son in spite of the fact that he knew that his father's death would be his own ruin. The loyalty which consists of not wishing the British army to go, and yet of doing everything to weaken the Government, trying to seize from it all the power of rule and undermining its influence in the hearts of the people, is a kind of loyalty I loathe. I had rather have an honest foe than an insidious and backbiting friend. Real loyalty tries to strengthen the Government and breathes a spirit of gratitude. The other loyalty is identical in its effects with the disloyalty of a wily enemy. We judge of men by their deeds and not by their words, and we judge of their loyalty by whether their actions tend to remove the soreness from the hearts of men or to aggravate it.

Coming now to the means adopted in this Congress agitation, the essential feature is that they do not confine their action to the educated classes, but make every effort to extend it to the ignorant. This tomfoolery about delegates necessitates it. Mass meetings are held and addressed by fiery orators; and inflammatory literature is circulated in the vernacular. Only the man who believes in the infinite gullibility of the Englishman can dare state that the masses in India can understand the question of the reform of the Legislative Councils, of which they have never even heard the name. As easily could a company of English rustics comprehend the philosophy of Kant. To understand how the Hindu is to govern India under the cloak of the British name by means of a representative system imported from England, the English with their swords standing by as the willing slaves of their rulers, is a conception sufficiently difficult to tax the intellectual resources of even a Calcutta graduate. One broad issue arises at once to the popular mind. British rule or Native rule? And when the English are abused and the grievances of the people are dwelt on, can there be any doubt on which side they will decide? To illustrate this by an example :—At a certain town a meeting was held, and as usual they secured as chairman (by what means I will not specify) a Mahomedan, so as to keep up the deceitful farce that the Mahomedans are with them. He was an uneducated nobleman, with nothing but the primitive ideas of rule in his head prevalent in the savage land from which he hails. They stood up and abused the English before him, one man calling English Assistant Collectors monkeys. What will be the effect on the mind of that wild and ignorant chief? I know of an unlettered Thakur Baron in a Native State who asks of his friends when the next mutiny is coming, being quite indifferent which side he takes, but longing for something to relieve the monotony of his dull life. I will not give his address lest the Congresswallahs should invite him to be chairman of a meeting in his country, or should send him a copy of the pamphlet to which I shall allude further on, when I shall bring more specific charges of disloyalty.

II.

In the first part of this discussion I pointed out that the very constitution of the National Congress was such that it was bound to foster a spirit of discontent and mutiny in the people ; that a Grievance Hall, as a permanent institution, would be like a running sore bringing all kinds of aches and pains to the body politic ; and that the delegate system, based as it was on popular support and popular discontent, was bound to encourage a kind of public speaking and literature, the object of which would be to picture in glowing colours the injustice of Government. And thus, however strong and however loyal the hands that controlled the movement, howcvcr much they might wish not to inflame discontent among the ignorant, it would be practically impossible to prevent the National Congress and its ramifications from becoming a deadly engine of sedition.

What then will be its effect when the leaders of this Congress, the authorised official heads, publish in their authorised official volumes, and throw broadcast over the land, as an example to their followers in every district, literature of an actively incendiary nature? At the end of the report of the National Congress is printed a pamphlet which, I am told, has been largely circulated in the vernacular, in which case a certain number of potential mutineers has probably been already created by it. I shall make some extracts from this poisonous tract, but I can, in so short a space, give no adequate notion of the amount of venom hidden in it. I request all who take an interest in public affairs, and in the future of this glorious country and of its gifted peoples, to purchase a copy of the report and study the tract for themselves. It represents a hypothetical conversation between a Congresswallah (a Maulvi !) and a peasant. The Congresswallah points to the difference in prosperity between two villages—one *Shamshpur*, which is owned jointly by the villagers, and another *Kambakthpur*, owned by an absentee Raja. The former is said to typify India as it would be under a native representative government, and the latter, India as it is under British rule. A vivid contrast is drawn between the prosperity of Shamshpur and the misery of Kambakthpur. Every misfortune from which our poor peasants suffer, whether removable by Government or beyond the resources of human power to cure—the poverty, the extortions of the money-lender, the oppression of the police, the ill-effects of canal water—are described with studied accuracy as ruining Kambakthpur, while from all of them Shamshpur is free. With such illusions did Jack Cade urge on his band of rebels. I will now quote :—

Maulvi Farid-ud-din :—"But how does your village thrive ?"

Rambaksh :—"How does it thrive? Why, Maulvi Sahib, you know that there never is a day but that there is some case from Kambakthpur in Court; that we are growing poorer and poorer; that land is going out of cultivation; that we have scarcely oxen enough to plough what we still till. Look down the street; why the houses are half of them nearly in ruins, and the two *abkari* shops that the *Sirkar* has set up here are always full. Even this *chopal*, built by our forefathers and so much needed for our meetings and our guests, is now in ruins. Look at Shamshpur. It is twice as populous as this *bustee* (village), and yet there is no *abkari* shop there, and the *lumbardar* says there never shall be, and so say they all. Thrive indeed! Of all the miserable places in this whole zila Kambakthpur is nearly one of the worst."

Thus the British Government is charged with making the people drunk by its liquor policy; to its door is laid the poverty of the peasantry; and regardless of facts, it is said that the poverty of the country is increasing and the land is passing out of cultivation.

Further on English officials, as a class, are thus described :—"They don't know the difference between a 6-anna crop and a 16-anna crop, and press in bad times for rent, so that we have to sell our cattle; they don't know who is reliable (*matbir*), and they make advances, when none ought to be given, to ne'er-do-weels that lose their money, and then say we are *all budmashes* (bad characters, rogues), and won't even give seed grain to the best of us, when times are such that we really need it. And then they are fussy and self-conceited, and won't hear a word from any of us. There was the old tank there, the Soorujkund, that from generation to generation used to irrigate half the village; that burst when I was a boy fifty years ago. Well, we wanted the Raja to repair this. It wouldn't have cost many hundred rupees, and the whole village knew from their forefathers how well it worked. But no! *Naib Sahib* knew better, he wouldn't listen to us. 'What you cattle-folk know? Hold your tongues.' He was all for new-fangled plans. He would bring a *kul* (channel) of the *Sirkari* canal to irrigate the village. We told him that canal water is cold, that our land lay low, that it would not do. But what was the use? 'What you cattle-folk know? Hold your tongues;' and so the *kul* was brought, and the first year it overflowed and swamped half the crops, and then when the water dried up the canal people came and measured up all the land, and made us pay tax for 'one watering.' A fine thing, seeing it had ruined our crops. But we had to pay, and now it is bringing the *reh* (a saline efflorescence) all over our best lands. The Raja pays no heed to us; his naibs understand nothing of our affairs. They order this and order that, press us for money in season and out of season, they know nothing of village matters themselves, and they won't hear a word from us because they think they are all-wise and we utter fools—and under such a system (*dastur*), how can a village be otherwise than ruined?"

Thus, even our benevolent efforts to avert famine by means of irrigation are used as a dagger wherewith to stab us. I will close my extracts with the following charming description of an English Collector, Mr. Zabardast :—

Rambaksh :—" Remember him? Ram, Ram, *'ska nam mut lo* (don't mention him), I bear his marks now (where I can't show them to you Maulvi Sahib), though it is twenty years ago. You see, his *lushkar* (camp) came to our village. There was no grass for the horses; the Collector shouted to the Tahsildar, who said Rambaksh was responsible. 'Oh,' said the Sahib, striking me with his whip, ' 'you are the son of a pig, the misbegotten (*suar ka bacha, haramzada*). I'll teach you how to attend to orders. Here, *khlassi* (tent-pitcher), tie him up and give him thirty *baints* (blows with a cane), and lay it well on.' Now the Tahsildar had never spoken a word to me about the matter. I tried to explain this, but the Sahib hit me over the mouth and face with his whip, shouting out 'hold your tongue. I'll teach you! Tie him up, tie him up, flog his life out;' and I was dragged away and flogged till I became insensible. It was a month before I could walk. Yes, he was a bad one; many Collectors have I known—some good, some indifferent—but this was the only real devil."

Now what does this mean, and what will it lead to? It means—if Government allows this sort of propaganda to go on—it means the massacre of Englishmen and their wives and children. For on what material is this seditious trash thrown? Not on the educated and cultured. Not on those who owe their means of livelihood to British rule, and who would be swept away at once if it went. Not on men who are afraid of fighting. The people of these Provinces are not cowards; they love a fight as well almost as an Englishman. We had examples at Delhi and Etawah. And some classes of these people, notably the Mahomedan and the Thakur, the most spirited and pugnacious, have lost terribly by the turn in the political kaleidoscope. Religious fanaticism is not yet dead. And the poverty of the whole Mahomedan community and of the noble families is so distressing, and their backwardness in English education is so great, that only a Government which was the slave of noise or doctrinaire theories would frame measures in disregard of it. Now if they are urged to dwell on their sorrows, which are invariably laid to the British Government, instead of trying to improve themselves by trade and education, the result will be that disloyalty will take its seat in their hearts. Do you think they will stop at reform of the Legislative Councils? And do you think the Congress people who have stirred up these passions can allay them? They would be blown away as butterflies in a hurricane.

The worst sufferers by a mutiny would be Mahomedans. As far as savagery goes both sides would have a good fling. At such a period men become fiends, and the innocent and the guilty, the strong and the defenceless, share the same fate. The English nation, on whose benevolence at home the Congresswallahs lay such stress, would forget all about constitutions and elective councils, and cry only for vengeance. But England would not lose her national existence, while the Mahomedan would be irretrievably ruined. This is why the Mahomedan leaders wish to keep their people from the whirlpool of political agitation. My revered chief, Sir Syed Ahmed, whose humble disciple in matters political I boast myself, has pointed this out clearly. No one has even grappled with his arguments, but in place of reason a shower of mud and abuse has been hurled at him ever since. He has been called selfish, foolish, childish and a flatterer. But the fact is people in other Provinces and of other nations can in no way understand the circumstances and feelings of the people here. The Bengali has made enormous progress under British rule; his political star is in the ascendant; how can he put himself in the position of the Musalman whose greatness is in the past and who sees ruin staring him in the face? If in spite of this he will disseminate his poisonous literature among Mahomedans, have not Mahomedan patriots a right to be angry? In Bengal, Madras and Bombay, there was no mutiny, though, if report be right, materials exist for one in the last of these Provinces. To people there it seems an unreality, a chimera. But it is far otherwise here. Our old men were middle aged in 1857. The *Bombay Gazette* urged the Mahomedans of the N.-W. P. to indulge in a little "wholesome grumbling," if they could find anything to grumble about. Pray how, if we start grumbling, are we to be sure that it will remain "wholesome?" There is plenty for Mahomedans to grumble at. This so-called self-Government of the municipalities, in which Mahomedans have been bound hand and foot and handed over to their rivals to be governed by them, is a case in point. An order just issued by the Bengal Government that all minor appointments are to be given by competitive examination—an order which will almost destroy the Mahomedan middle-class which cannot for one generation at least acquire English education sufficient to compete with others, is another. But rather than bring these things forward and create a popular agitation, we will submit to them as the lesser evil. Another Syed Ahmed, the great Wahabi, and Maulvi Ismail, his supporter, raised a great popular agitation, but urged their followers never to attack the British. They fought the Sikhs, but after that what took place? To every thoughtful Mahomedan the idea of another mutiny is as horrible, more horrible I believe than to an Englishman; and to every Musalman lady more dreadful even than to an English lady.

I have written the above on the supposition that the promoters of this movement have no desire of raising a storm, but are doing it unwittingly, not knowing the country. But this is by no means as certain as it at first sight appears. In the report of the Congress, after many eloquent harangues on urging forward "the chariot of India's destined development," there comes with a sense of infinite relief a speech by a man, Babu Ambica Charan Muzamdar, who had the courage to express opinions distasteful to the majority. He said:—"There is a kind of maniacal writing in many of the petty Vernacular papers that would qualify, and should qualify, the writers for prison diet." But he was shouted down. This is a small incident. It would not be fair to press it too far. Of very much more serious account as showing the *conscious* drift of the movement is a pamphlet written by Mr. Hume, "The Father of the Congress," entitled *The Star in the East.* At the close are printed some articles from the *Indian Mirror*, evidently written by the same hand; but whether written by him or not, printed and sanctioned by him in this pamphlet. These letters are actively and consciously seditious. No one but a madman would have written them if he did not wish to bring the people to the verge of rebellion. I make the following quotation:—

"We again quote Mr. Payne:—'The settlers (at Cape Colony) petitioned for Representative Government in 1841, but their claims were neglected (*they took no measures to make themselves disagreeable*), and so little attention was paid to their wishes that the Home Government, when the Australians refused to take any more convicts, determined to make the Cape a penal settlement, and in 1849 despatched a shipload of convicts to Cape Town. The colonists, who were resolved to make a stand, rose in arms and refused to allow them to be landed. This incident fixed their claims on public attention, and in the next year (1850) the Governor was empowered to summon a constituent council for the purpose of settling a more acceptable form of government.'

"Full responsible Government was then conceded, and though their path, in other ways, has been beset with thorns, this was the end of the colonists' troubles with their Government.

"Now, can anything show more clearly than this simple, unvarnished story that the whole secret of eliciting reform at the hands of our good Lord and Master, John Bull, is to make oneself disagreeable? You may apparently complain and petition *ad infinitum*; thus did the Canadians, the Australians and the Cape, but they took nothing by their motions; they might shout until they were hoarse, but until they began to kick, to fight, or evince a readiness to do so—until, in fact, they began to make themselves disagreeable in good earnest—no one paid the slightest attention to them.

"Very clearly we have to make ourselves disagreeable, and please God, as time goes on, we will do so, and no mistake. But there are ways and ways of doing things; we do not approve of a resort to arms. We shall not break either the laws of God or man. We shall work within both constitutional and common law and local law limits, but we shall nevertheless hope to make ourselves ultimately so stupendously disagreeable as to force even our claims on public attention, and so secure those modifications in the existing form of the administration which are essential to the prosperity of India, and the well-being of her now greatly depressed and suffering population."

He also quotes Canada as rising in arms, praises the Canadians for it, and says Indians must take this lesson to heart, but not rise in arms. However, if freedom of the Press and the right to agitate be interfered with, he says:—"*We* also may begin to think of sterner measures to vindicate our rights." Is this direct incentive to mutiny or not? Does it or does it not tend to a repetition of those scenes at which the whole world shuddered? He brings forward examples of colonies which have gained the identical proposals of the National Congress after, and only after, an appeal to arms. He lays the greatest emphasis on this again and again, and tells his followers to take the lesson of the colonies to heart. He tells the people of India to take the first steps towards this rebellion, and to make themselves "stupendously disagreeable." He says there are other ways of accomplishing this without an appeal to arms, but he does not say what those ways are. Then he says it would be wrong for Indians to mutiny; but he does not explain why it was right in the colonists, as he positively asserts it was, and would be wrong in the people of India. Now

Mr. Hume may wish us to believe that the sentence, telling the people of India not to appeal to arms, is a proof that there is nothing seditious in his intentions. It is nothing of the sort. To have ended the reasoning with the natural conclusion, an exhortation to revolt, would have been absolute treason, and would have brought Mr. Hume within the compass of the law. Therefore he gives all the steps of the reasoning and leaves his readers to draw the right conclusion, himself cleverly ending up with an illogical statement by which he seeks to evade the direct charge of treason. No man who really wished to keep the people quiet, and to dispel notions of revolt, would have held up the picture of countries which had gained what they wanted by revolt. A man who wants to cure a drunkard does not place a glass of brandy on the table before him, deliver an oration on the delight of its flavour, tell him he can have it by stretching out his hand, and that many people have derived the greatest benefit from drinking brandy, but that under present circumstances it would be wiser if he abstained.

Furthermore, he insinuates that the people ought to mutiny if freedom of the Press and the right to agitate be removed. Why freedom of the Press and the right to agitate in particular? No one but an Englishman would have singled out those two things as the only causes justifying a rebellion. There are many things an Oriental cares infinitely more about—his religion, for example. And would not anyone, Oriental or not, care more about the alleged poverty of the country—not to mention the castigations of Mr. Zabardast? A Press Act would be no grievance to the people in Kambakthpur; may they not rise for their many grievances which he is so careful to point out to them? And even if a Press Act be the greatest evil the people of India could suffer, is it not dangerous morality to teach them that they have the right to rebel? Perhaps, indeed, Government will not carry its mania for license of the Press to such an exent as to allow active incentives to revolt. Will Mr. Hume then be ready to stand by his words? Let him head the Congress and die the death of a martyr, with as many Congresswallahs as he can get to stand by him! But let him not stir up the Mahomedan and the Thakur to their ruin.

All this that I have said may appear to English ears very unwarranted by the circumstances. I don't think it will so appear to the ears of my Hindustani countrymen. Everything looks quiet and peaceable. Popular agitation flourishes in England and nothing bad takes place. Yes; but England is not a conquered people under foreign rule. And, moreover, the people there is king. Popular agitation is nothing more than the working of the king's mind. The constitution at once brings into effect the people's wishes. But to talk of a "constitutional agitation" when there is, and can be, no constitution, is a perversion of language. And agitation without a constitution to work it off on is the prelude of bloodshed. Look at Ireland. And popular agitation in India will inevitably end in its becoming another Ireland on a much larger scale. We live apart from the people, and we take little trouble to see what is going on. The thing is still in its infancy and could be checked. The virus has not yet spread far in these Provinces. But after a time it will be very difficult to check it. It is no proof that because things are smooth and quiet there is no danger. How was the Mutiny of 1857 ushered in? The Anglo-Indian world up to the hour when the great tragedy burst upon them was busily amusing itself as best it can in this country with social nothings. And what were the causes of this Mutiny? The generally assigned cause is that the people feared their religion was about to be touched by Government. This National Congress is not a religious business. But religion is not the only thing which affects men. Poverty is as strong a provocative of crime as anything else. Mr. Dadabhai Nowroji is diligently trying to prove that India is growing poorer. This can produce no harm in his own community, who live like princes and are a thousand times as rich as they used to be. But on nations which are really impoverished it may produce deadly effects. A political cause is also given for the great Mutiny—the annexation of Oudh. If the passions of the people be stirred up about politics, there is no reason why there should not be a mutiny. The soldiery will readily imbibe the sentiments, and then all will be up. Mr. Hume boasted that he and his organisation could reach the soldiers and fill them with their sentiments and ideas. The people will get ready and wait for a favourable opportunity. If there be a single battle lost in a fight with Russia, this will be taken as the signal, and the whole of India will be aflame.

These are my reasons for believing that this popular agitation will, if allowed to go on, ultimately cause a mutiny. I will point out further on how, as it seems to me, this agitation may be checked.

III.

In the two previous discussions I laid down the proposition that popular political agitation—which has now for the first time manifested itself in India on a large scale—will, unless checked, presently throw the country into a most terrible state of anarchy, and deliver it a prey to murder and rapine. And that as regards this particular agitation of the National Congress, the methods employed are so noxious, characterised by a spirit of incendiarism so rash and so reckless (more especially in the English agitators), that it has become imperatively necessary to grapple with the evil in good earnest, and to apply radical remedies for this dangerous disease.

To treat it effectively, we must first see clearly its cause. I believe that the cause is entirely due to ourselves, and that its remedy lies in our own hands, if we can but overcome our own national defects. The cause is the combination of two characteristics of British politics—*first*, being slow to remedy grievances and grant favours when not clamoured for; *second*, being easily moved when sufficient clamour is raised. Now, the fact to be laid hold of is, that while these principles are suited to politics in England, in India they are fatal. I will begin with the *second*. We indulge in the gigantic fallacy of supposing that yielding to popular agitation assuages it. Exactly the opposite is true. For years and years the great standing grievance of the Native Press has been the low age for admission to the Civil Service. At last a Public Service Commission is made, which reports that the age should be raised to 23. How much gratitude is expressed? That grievance is pigeon-holed, and with increased energy they are calling for larger concessions. We are so indoctrinated with our English theories as to what is sound government, borrowed from English history and from daily English politics, that we have the greatest possible difficulty in adapting ourselves to a country where the people, Anglo-Indian as well as Native, is not ruler but ruled. What is the height of wisdom in the one country becomes the height of folly in the other. The methods of democracy are as pernicious in India as those of despotism would be in England. The English politician has no greater difficulty than to shake himself free of his democratic predilections. As the Oriental is tempted to flatter the king or high official, so the Englishman flatters the populace. And we commit the error when we come to India of trying to flatter that small section of the people which talks, instead of governing the whole people with firmness, impartiality, and generosity. An eminent Anglo-Indian official in London recently took to flattering even the National Congress before its lustre was impaired. Our weak side has been discovered and worked on. The least indication of measures unfavourable to the class that commands the Press has been met with volleys of abuse. Instead of snapping our fingers at this abuse, we quail at it. Government treads gingerly and cautiously, whereas if it were well informed of the people it would march boldly. Newspapers and public meetings have a ludicrously strong effect on the English mind. There is unfortunately some truth in Mr. Hume's remark that John Bull is not easily moved without a clamour; and the impression is vastly exaggerated on the native mind, because the people who never cease clamouring happen to be those who are best educated in English, and the prosperity due to their education is attributed to the abuse. In this the real danger lies. And to cure this defect of ours—the tendency to give in to agitation—must be our first effort.

On the other hand, as the necessary complement of this, it is the part of the Indian Government to show such favours from time to time as she can without danger to the stability of her rule; such acts as a loving father would do for his sons. She should dispense her favours royally; her gifts should emanate from her own Imperial pleasure; there should be no kind of appearance that they have been extorted from her; nor should they smack of stinginess or meanness. Now, it too often happens that the favours we do the people appear as no favours at all, but merely as concessions to popular demand, or as devices for saving money. Government appears to be in terror of the Native Press. The people who by their pens and ink-bottles exercise this terrorism often mock at Government for being afraid of them. The other races look on in amazement. Nor should the gifts of Government bear the signs of stinginess and of meanness, or be tainted with the flavour of race partiality. I will give an example to illustrate my meaning. We should never have been such fools as to have reduced the pay and emoluments of the high posts given to Natives if we had realised how completely in the eyes of the Natives this robbed them of their grace, showing Government not as a generous Queen but as a mean huckster. If economy was our object we might have tried other methods; but not this. The people of England gladly spend half a million a year for the Royal expenses. Would the people of India grudge a few thousand rupees to complete the honour of those few men of their own blood who enjoy high posts? We have yet to learn how to give favours so as to win loyalty.

Hence the method I would suggest is that we should make it a rule never to give in to agitation, and the stronger the agitation, the more disloyal its tendency, the harsher and the more stubborn should we be. On the other hand, we should be only too ready to do what we can, when the people make their requests in a quiet and gentlemanly way without stirring up discontent. Better still, we should of our own motion grant them favours. But most important of all, we should show in a manner unmistakable and patent to all that those nations which are loyal and which refuse to hamper the hands of Government gain and do not lose by their loyalty. To neglect them, but to listen to the noisy voices of the ungrateful, would be shameful ; it would encourage ingratitude and discourage gratitude; create sedition and dispel loyalty ; it would be political insanity. If we follow these methods, agitation will then very soon die a natural death. But as long as we adhere to our present policy it will be very difficult to keep it within bounds. The people finding it pay, and intent only on an immediate gain, will stir up sedition, disloyalty, and discontent, regardless of the future dreadful consequences.

But it will be said :—"How are we to give favours unless we know the wants of the people? Shall we not offend rather than please them by our mistakes? And how are we to know the wants of the people unless by the Press and by Congresses the people indulge in a little 'wholesome grumbling.'" The answer involves a statement of what I regard as the radical weakness of our Empire. If the Indian Government cannot by its public servants know with absolute certainty the wants of the people, or if, knowing them, it has not the generosity, so far as practicable, to grant them, then we are unfit to hold the Empire. At present Englishmen, as a rule, live apart from the Natives.

It is a more comfortable way of finding out what the people want to peruse a newspaper at *chota-haziri*, or study a Congress report. One has been accustomed to it at home, and why should one not do it here, without the bother and inconvenience and effort of mixing in Oriental society? The consequence is, the Press befools us to the top of our bent. Its deliberate object is not to represent the people, but to represent a party. This is human nature. The fact is there are loads of things the people feel. They feel first and foremost our supercilious contempt for them; they feel aggravated and disgusted by the invidious distinctions we make between the pay of English and Native officials in the same posts; they feel the want of a military career. If we lived among them we should feel it more. We should know what to do, and should do it. But it is objected that our hands are tied by the Government at home which exerts, and will continue to exert, a well-meant and most disastrous influence on Indian statesmen. True. But this is only one of the difficulties to be overcome. With a body of men possessing the full confidence of the people, minutely conversant with their ways of thought, and with a good literary training, we could easily keep that section of the British public which takes an interest in Indian affairs sufficiently well-informed to prevent foolish interference. But for this we must know the people far better than we do now. I firmly believe that if we go on recruiting our Civil Service as we are now doing, the

Empire has not got a long life to run. We should bring out men at a mature age, men of the best University education and the highest intellectual culture, men who have seen the world and know that India is not the only country in which men are selfish and are actuated by every kind of motive, honourable and dishonourable. We should bring out the very best and ablest men that England produces. For we shall need them. The first thing to be done is to raise the age of competition. If the best men will not compete, the salaries and other emoluments of the posts must be increased. We have to produce the future statesmen of India, and to economise at the expense of having foolish statesmen would be the most suicidal economy. If competitive examination anyhow will not give us the best men, we must invent another means. The existence of an Empire is at stake, and it cannot be sacrificed to fads. Then every man who comes out must do so on the distinct understanding that he must live among the people, and make himself so much of an Oriental that by the vibration of his own feelings he can say how the measures of Government will affect his fellow-men. The men who built up our Empire did this, but now-a-days a man who tries to do it is looked on by a large number of his contrymen as a contemptible madman. I do not hesitate to say that the conceptions afloat in ordinary English society as to the native character are grotesquely absurd and unjust. I am not making any reflection on the honour, the integrity, and the high character of the Anglo-Indian community. I believe it would be impossible in England to find in any class a better body of men. The notions prevalent there about us are most unfair. The talk about Englishmen in India losing their good qualities is nonsense—rather they gain a certain tough fibre of manliness and hardihood. But my complaint is that we do not cure a defect common to Englishmen everywhere—our insularity. The effort, I admit, is too great for the average man. We do not require it as a duty from the engineer or the doctor. But from those who are to be rulers of the country, the guardians of our national greatness, we have a right to demand it. But there are difficulties, you say. Yes, there are difficulties; but with the history of our Empire before us are we to shirk difficulties? There are in this no difficulties which an Englishman, who sets his mind to it, cannot overcome. The countrymen of Gordon and of Raja Brooke have no right to talk about difficulties. The honour of our country demands it: that is enough. There are thousands of men ready to die for her: are there none ready to live for her? To know the people, and to be so trusted by them that they will open out to us the inmost recesses of their hearts; to see them daily; to come to love them as those who have in their nature but an average share of affection cannot help loving them, when they know them well—this is our ideal for the Indian Civilian. Some Englishmen act up to this ideal: in the early days of our rule several did.

If it become the normal thing the Indian Empire will be built upon a rock so that nothing can shake it. Agitation and sedition will vanish as ugly shadows. Had it existed in 1857 the crash would not have come. If now we can bring it about that we have a thousand Englishmen in this country who, from the ardour of their patriotism, their passionate pride in the glory of our unrivalled country which has encircled the world with its civilisation, will force themselves to spend their days of exile in the society, sometimes uncongenial, of their Eastern brothers, knowing them as they know themselves, then India will be linked to us by indissoluble ties, and the name of England will remain for ever in the world's history as having accomplished a feat unparalleled for difficulty and benevolence. We may then banish the nightmare of mutiny. But if we continue in our supercilious contempt for the people, if we remain indifferent to the effects of agitation as being beneath our notice, then the day may again come when society will be horror-struck by the grim presence of living tragedy.

NOTES.

1. *On preventive measures.*—The remedy I have suggested in the last essay for political agitation is not sufficient by itself I think to prevent disaster. Before it would have time to operate the crash would probably arrive. It is necessary to protect the ignorant populace from the deadly effect of the irrational discontent that is every day being propagated with increasing energy. This can only be done (1) by preventing the spread of literature of a seditious tendency, (2) by forbidding public meetings at which incendiary speeches are made. The business of statesmen is to foresee impending evils and to avert them. They have to prevent the massacre of their countrymen and the ruin of India, however unable public opinion may be to understand the necessity of their measures.

2. *On raising the age of competition for the Civil Service.*—I think we made a fatal mistake in reducing, within recent years, the age of competition for the Indian Civil Service. On two accounts is it prejudicial to bring out youths instead of men. In the first place, we do not get men of anything like so high an average of ability as we should if the maximum age were 24 instead of 19. A tract was written some years ago by Mr. Oscar Browning, Fellow of King's College, Cambridge, and Lecturer on History in the University of Cambridge, prophecying danger for the Indian Empire from the fact that the young men preparing at Cambridge for the Indian Civil Service were, as a rule, far from being in the front rank of University students. And yet there is no doubt that many of the best University men would gladly accept posts in the Indian Civil Service if they had the chance of doing so after taking

their degrees. Fellows of Colleges and the most brilliant students compete for posts in the Home Civil Service, posts carrying not one-half the pay, nor one-twentieth the political influence of those in the Indian Civil Service, nor offering to ambition those glorious positions of autocratic rulership over Provinces as large and as populous as the United Kingdom. The reason why these men do not compete now for the Indian Civil Service is that most clever boys of 16 or 17 will not sacrifice a University career and the indefinite but splendid prospects they imagine it opens for them, and exile themselves in a country in which they take no interest. But when, after attaining high honors at the University, they discover how choked are all the avenues of professional life, and that their only chance of gaining a livelihood is by dragging out miserable years of penury at the English bar, or by accepting an obscure under-mastership, or gaining a precarious income with no prospects by lecturing under the University Extension scheme, or teaching some rich man's son ; they would jump at a career, which not only gave them a substantial, though not a lordly, income, enabling them to marry the women they loved or looked forward to loving, but opened out a magnificent sphere of usefulness for the man of action, and an unbounded region of research for the scholar. By that time their latent interest in political, social, and every kind of question that delights the student, would have been called forth ; and the gratification of their ambition or curiosity would counteract the repugnance to exile in this magnificent old country.

The second reason why it would be advantageous to bring men out at a maturer age is that they would be better fitted for their work when they came. It is a mistake to cut short a man's education when he has before him tasks of such gigantic difficulty as fall to the Indian administrator. There is a danger, which all who have experienced it will bear witness to, of intellectual stagnation in the lonely stations in which many Anglo-Indians are obliged to pass the best years of their lives; and the best way to avert this is by the prolonged active exercise of the intellect in Europe before coming to India. Moreover, the utmost breadth of culture is required to give men those cosmopolitan instincts which are needed for appreciating the Natives of India and their civilization. Men who know Europe well will not be surprised at every human failing they find in the East, and suppose it has no counterpart in the West. But people who have seen but little of the world are apt to judge of a nation's qualities by comparing the individuals they meet with their own friends, and not with mankind at large. I do not believe that the young men coming out in the Indian Civil Service are equal to the older ones who are about to retire. If this be true there can be no more melancholy foreboding for the Indian Empire. The Indian Empire has been made by the Civil Service: its future rests in their hands. They furnish our statesmen, or their advisers. They hold power and are the embodiment of the British name in every corner of the continent. Measures of reform emanate from them. Nothing can be done without them; everything with them. To give us her best sons is the supreme duty that England owes India.
